ANCIENT TEXT MESSAGES OF THE YORÙBÁ *BÀTÁ* DRUM

Ancient Text Messages of the Yorùbá *Bàtá* Drum

Cracking the Code

AMANDA VILLEPASTOUR
The MIM, Phoenix, Arizona, USA

ASHGATE

Published by
Ashgate Publishing Limited
Wey Court East
Union Road
Farnham
Surrey, GU9 7PT
England

Ashgate Publishing Company
Suite 420
101 Cherry Street
Burlington
VT 05401–4405
USA

www.ashgate.com

British Library Cataloguing in Publication Data
Villepastour, Amanda.
    Ancient text messages of the Yorùbá *bàtá* drum : cracking the code. – (SOAS musicology series)
    1. Yorùbá (African people) – Music – History and criticism. 2. *Bàtá*. 3. Drum language. 4. Yorùbá language. 5. Music and language.
    I. Title II. Series III. University of London. School of Oriental and African Studies.
    786.9'216296333–dc22

Library of Congress Cataloging-in-Publication Data
Villepastour, Amanda, 1958–
    Ancient text messages of the Yorùbá *bàtá* drum : cracking the code / Amanda Villepastour.
        p. cm. – (SOAS musicology series)
    Includes bibliographical references.
    ISBN 978–0–7546–6753–7 (hardcover : alk. paper)
    1. *Bàtá* music – Nigeria – History and criticism. 2. Drum language – Nigeria.
    3. Yorùbá (African people) – Music – History and criticism.
    I. Title.
    ML1038.B38V56 2009
    786.9'20896333–dc22   2009016963

The AfroRomanU fonts used in this work are available from www.linguistsoftware.com

ISBN 9780754667537

Mixed Sources
Product group from well-managed forests and other controlled sources
www.fsc.org Cert no. SA-COC-1565
© 1996 Forest Stewardship Council
FSC

Printed and bound in Great Britain by
MPG Books Group, UK

Contents

List of Illustrations

List of Tables

List of Music Examples

The symbol ⊙ indicates that the example is also an audio example on the CD that accompanies this book. The number refers to the track number on the CD.

---

* Examples A.II.1 through to A.II.20 are audio examples that can be heard on the CD that accompanies this book. Please refer to Appendix II for musical transcriptions, texts and translations, along with CD track listings.

List of CD Examples

Acknowledgements

I am grateful to the friends and colleagues whose patience, hard work and generosity contributed to the completion of this volume. The first acknowledgement must go to my research collaborators, master drummer Chief Alhaji Rábíù Àyándòkun and information scientist and linguist 'Túndé Adégbọlá, who both took leave from their work in Nigeria to undertake one-month residencies at SOAS. As always, I am grateful to my friend Táíwò Abímbọ́lá, who collected and translated oral literature and drum texts, recorded *bàtá* performances and worked hard on the translations. The CD was recorded by Jeremy Glasgow and Michel Massimo and edited, mixed and mastered by Michel. I am appreciative to both sound engineers for their time and patience above and beyond the call of duty. Acknowledgement goes to Professor Akínwùnmí Ìṣọ̀lá, who Adégbọlá and I consulted with several language queries. Thanks to Professor Michael Marcuzzi, who is always a brilliant sounding board and source of information. Michael made a significant contribution to my study with a conference paper presented at the Society of Ethnomusicology (2004). Michael also introduced me to *Transcribe!* software, saving me countless hours in the transcription process. Thank you also to Emem Adégbọlá, who assisted with the graphics. I am indebted to the AHRC Research Centre for funding my research fellowship (2006–2007) and financing the CD in this volume. Last but certainly not least, thank you to Professor Keith Howard, director of the AHRC Research Centre, who supervized my fellowship and the compilation of this volume, and Andrea Hector-Watkins for her administrative support during the project.

Introduction

The *bàtá* is a Yorùbá drumming tradition at least five centuries old and is part of a spiritual tradition that predates the introduction of Islam and Christianity into Yorùbáland. Although *bàtá* is a dying drumming tradition and is less known than the more popular Yorùbá *dùndún* drum, it is of growing cultural importance as *òrìṣà* religion and interest in Yorùbá cultural traditions grow in the African diaspora and beyond. Regardless of the pressures bearing down on the *bàtá* tradition in Nigeria, this volume documents its remarkable speech surrogacy technology, along with the unique vernacular developed by Àyàn (born) drummers, which they refer to as *ẹnà bàtá*.

The research presented in this volume derives from a collaboration between Rábíù Àyándòkun, a Yorùbá master drummer, 'Túndé Adégbọlá, a Yorùbá linguist and information scientist, and myself, an ethnomusicologist. For almost a decade, the three of us have been having informal conversations with one another about the *bàtá's* extraordinary powers to communicate with people and with spiritual beings. This volume formalizes those years of conversation, friendships and research, and presents the first detailed study of the *bàtá's* utterances.

The Research

I was introduced to Rábíù Àyándòkun by the Yorùbá ethnomusicologist Akin Euba in 1996. Thanks to Euba, Àyándòkun and I have been working together since 1999, both in his home town of Ẹ̀rìn-Òṣun in southwest Nigeria and in the UK, where he has become a regular visitor. I first met 'Túndé Adégbọlá at the launch of one of his own film productions at the October Gallery in London in 1997. Our very first conversation was about the *bàtá's* talking capacity. When I told Adégbọlá that I was undertaking research about the *bàtá's* drum language, he looked at me in amazement and said, 'I didn't know that the *bàtá* can talk!' Like many contemporary Yorùbá people, Adégbọlá believed that Yorùbá surrogate speech was within the exclusive domain of the *dùndún* drum, which was featured in the film he was premiering, *Ṣaworo Idẹ*. Since that first conversation, Adégbọlá has shared my research interest about the *bàtá's* surrogate speech capacity, and whenever we met in the UK or Nigeria in subsequent years, we embarked on animated conversations about drum communications.

Over the past few years, Àyándòkun and Adégbọlá have become acquainted with one another through their engagement with Yorùbá traditions and through their research work with me. Indeed, Àyándòkun and Adégbọlá have since worked together on a film for cinema, *Agogo Èèwò* (2002), produced by Mainframe, the production company in which Adégbọlá is a partner. Through undertaking a fellowship at SOAS (funded by the AHRC) from October 2006 to August 2007, I have had the opportunity to organize a formal research collaboration between the three of us. We have combined our diverse expertise as ritual drummer, language and communication scientist and ethnomusicologist to elucidate the *bàtá's* system of speech surrogacy.

This volume presents a CD with drumming performances of *ìlù òrìṣà* (spiritual rhythms), *oríkì* (praise poetry), *òwe* (proverbs) and selected words and sentences that have both generated and illustrate several aspects of my findings. The transcriptions presented in this volume relate to the recordings on the CD and provide both the source material and examples for the analysis in the text.

Numbering System

The figures, tables, illustrations and musical examples presented in this volume are numbered in four different categories, according to the chapter or appendix in which they appear, followed by a decimal point and Arabic numeral indicating the order within the chapter or appendix. For example, Illustration 1.2 is the second illustration in Chapter 1, while Example 3.3 is the third transcription in Chapter 3 and Table 4.3 is the third table in Chapter 4. Examples in the appendices will be identified by a capital A (denoting appendix) and a roman numeral (denoting which appendix). Hence Example AII.15 directs the reader to the fifteenth example in Appendix II. All illustrations and examples in the preface are numbered in lowercase roman numerals.

The Recordings

Àyándòkun was invited to the UK as a SOAS artist-in-residence in March–April 2007. During this period he gave me lessons, engaged in interviews and less formal conversations, and made recordings in the SOAS recording studio. These recordings were not designed to reflect commonplace *bàtá* performance practice, but were crafted to elicit research data that corresponds with the musical material generated by my lessons with Àyándòkun between 1999 and 2006. The examples on the CD included with this volume have been edited and compiled to illustrate material in the text and transcriptions.

There have been very few commercial releases of Yorùbá *bàtá* drumming. Available recordings include three Folkways releases, *Drums of the Yoruba of Nigeria* (1953), *Yoruba Bata Drums Elewe Music and Dance* (1980) and *Yoruba Drums from Benin, West Africa* (1996) plus a more recent CD *AyanAgalú* (2001) from independent label Graviton Records. The Folkways recordings are not exclusively *bàtá* drumming, and none of these four recordings include concentrated studies of the *bàtá*. The transcriptions and explanations of the recorded material on the CD with this volume will help listeners make sense of these earlier *bàtá* recordings, which, due to their rhythmic complexity and production limitations, can sound like a cacophony to the uninformed listener.

Recorded examples cited in the text will be indicated by the symbol ☉. Hence (☉ 37) would direct the reader to track 37 of the CD. The CD in this volume presents clear, in some ways laboratory representations of *bàtá* drumming. Rather than recording an ensemble of three musicians playing three drums – an option that was not available to us due to the lack of *bàtá* performers in the UK – Àyándòkun has overdubbed all of the parts himself. While the minimum ensemble would be comprised of the lead drum, *ìyáàlù*, the second drum, *omele abo*, and the small accompanying drum, *omele akọ* (see Illustration 1.1), and the three drummers would normally be mobile in a ceremonial context, Àyándòkun sat in controlled studio conditions wearing headphones and playing along with his own performances. This was a break from performance practice but the outcome nevertheless sounds like a live ensemble on several of the tracks.

The actual rhythms and drummed texts were carefully planned by Àyándòkun and me in order to present appropriate examples of the *bàtá's* repertoire. We drew from three main repertoires: *òwe* (proverbs), *oríkì* (praise poetry) and *ìlù òrìsà* (devotional rhythms). We recorded a list of twenty-three proverbs (*òwe*) on three different kinds of Yorùbá talking drum (*bàtá*, *omele mẹ́ta* and *dùndún*) in three different takes. However, one would never hear *òwe* strung together in the manner one hears them consecutively on the CD. In a real performance, the drummer's choices would be dictated by the personalities present and the dynamic social situation. Likewise, the *oríkì* and *òrìsà* rhythms are recorded in a succession that does not exemplify performance practice. We made a choice to record the basic *ìlù òrìsà* rhythms with a minimum of variations, as these can obscure the rhythmic patterns and render the pieces somewhat impenetrable for the novice listener. Àyándòkun chose to remove the brass bells (*sawaro*) from the lead drums (the *ìyáàlu bàtá* and the *ìyáàlù dùndún*), so as not to obscure the subtle hand strokes, which would be easier to perceive in a live performance or with audio-visual recordings. Such aural clarity is simply not possible when recording a mobile *bàtá* ensemble, where it is inevitably difficult to hear some of the parts (most particularly the lower-pitched skins, which are the most important 'talkers').

In yet another break from tradition, Àyándòkun recorded voice-overs of the drum texts after he recorded the drumming tracks. This assisted the transcription process and provided some material to help the listener follow the texts, which are normally rendered instrumentally (☉ 22 & 23). Àyándòkun also recorded sixteen *oríkì* where the drummed segments are interpolated with the parallel spoken segments, which would never happen in a performance context (☉ 12–21). He also recorded the *oríkì* with *ẹnà*, the coded spoken language of *bàtá* drummers (☉ 39 & 41). Although Yorùbá dancers will sometimes chant along with a drum text they recognize, it is not normative for performers to utter the drum texts as a performance practice.

As this volume makes a comparison of the speech surrogacy systems of the *bàtá* and *dùndún*, the recordings also include some *dùndún* examples (☉ 33, 34, 35, 37). (See Research Methods in Appendix I for more information about how I made the recordings and transcriptions.)

The final mixes on the CD are also not intended to be representative of performance practice. The two largest drums (*ìyáàlù* and *omele abo*) have two heads with highly contrasting sounds, one mellow and slightly sustained (the *ojú òjò*), the other loud and high-pitched with high transients and a fast decay (the *ṣáṣá*). We have panned the different heads (as illustrated in Illustration i.i) to help the listener separate the interlocking parts.

The recording is in stereo. The deepest sound is the *èjìn*, which is actually an *ìyáàlù* but is tuned below the leading *ìyáàlù* and plays only a rhythmic role, usually with its low tone on the first beat of the cycle (every two bars). The *èjìn* is only played on ☉ 1 and 32, and is panned in the middle. The second deepest sound, the *ojú òjò* (larger skin) of the *ìyáàlù*, is panned slightly left, while the *ojú òjò* of the *omele abo* (the higher-pitched skin, approximately an octave and a fifth higher than the *èjìn*) is panned slightly right. The three large skins of the *èjìn*, *ìyáàlù* and *omele abo* in this particular ensemble (☉ 1) are tuned roughly to a major triad, with the *omele abo* up an octave. As it is the two *ṣáṣá* of the *omele akọ* and the *ṣáṣá* of the two lead drums that are most difficult to distinguish, I have endeavoured to separate them as much as possible by panning the *ìyáàlù ṣáṣá* hard left, the *omele abo ṣáṣá* hard right, and the *omele akọ ṣáṣá* towards the centre.

The levels in the final mix are different from what Àyándòkun would have preferred to hear as a normal performance mix, but I have endeavoured to help the listener separate the parts and extract the talking skins rather than represent performance levels. The *ìyáàlù* dominates in the mix, as most of the analysis centres around how the *ìyáàlù* encodes speech. I have raised the level of the two *ojú òjò* (large skins) of the *ìyáàlù* and *omele abo* and lowered the comparative level of the rhythmic drum, the *omele akọ* (which usually dominates the overall sound), in order to push the two talking drums into the aural foreground.

The Musical Transcriptions

The transcriptions presented in this volume are designed to be descriptive and have been made for the purpose of analysis. Although they are not intended to be a prescriptive guide to playing the *bàtá*, an interesting by-product of the work is that musically literate drummers will, in fact, be able to use the information and material presented in this volume to make sense of a very difficult musical repertoire. One can begin learning the texts and rhythms represented by the transcriptions and recordings, which would provide the perfect preparation for studying with a master such as Àyándòkun.

The transcriptions are, at best, an approximation of the performances on the CD. Àyándòkun rarely plays the rigid, 'straight' quavers one sees in the scores, and

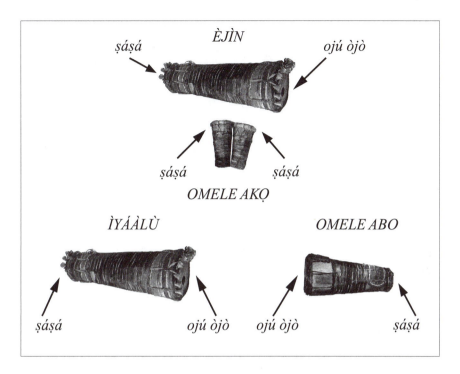

Illustration i.i.   Panning of the *bàtá* ensemble on the recordings

characteristically plays with varying degrees of microrhythmic shifts, although he sometimes shifts the rhythm forward as much as a quaver (e.g. *òwe* 6 ☉ 1) or moves outside of the pulse towards rapid renderings in free rhythm, only to snap back into the pulse. Such examples may sound like performance mistakes to a first-time listener, but they are in fact complex rhythmic performances that are very challenging to represent with conventional notation. Attempting to produce transcriptions that illustrate these microrhythmic shifts and phrase displacements would likely be unintelligible to the reader, so I have left the transcriptions on the pulse.

The *oríkì* are played in 'free speech time' rather than over a regular pulse. Hence the rhythmic organization of the transcriptions is approximately spaced with stemless note heads as the analysis is focussed on the strokes and their representation of speech tones in a broad rhythmic scheme.

The Notation

The *ìyáàlù* and *omele abo ojú òjò* use several kinds of hand strokes (see Illustrations i.ii–i.vi). The open tone is played by striking the edge of the *ojú òjò* and letting the fingers bounce off the skin. To produce the mute tone, the hand stays on the

Illustrations i.ii–i.vi: top left – *ìyáàlù* open; top right – *ìyáàlù* mute; middle – *ìyáàlù* slap; bottom left – *omele abo* open; bottom right – *omele abo* mute.

skin and damps the sound, producing a slightly higher fundamental frequency. For the slap tone, the hand moves towards the centre of the drum and the finger tips produce a high sound. The *bílálà* is a flexible raw hide beater that is used to strike the *ṣáṣá*, which is not played with the hands in the style of *bàtá* playing of Àyándòkun (see Illustration 1.2). As indicated in Example i.ii and i.iii, each of the *ojú òjò* tones can be played simultaneously with the *bílálà* stroke on the *ṣáṣá*.

I have chosen to adapt five-line stave notation for the transcriptions. For the two-headed drums, *ìyáàlù* and *omele abo*, I have used a two-line percussion stave with the bottom line representing the lower-pitched *ojú òjò* (right hand) and the top line representing the higher-pitched *ṣáṣá* (left hand). All stem directions are upward, regardless of the position of the stave, for uniformity. The strokes of the *ìyáàlù* are notated in Example i.i.

Example i.i.   Notation of the *ìyáàlù* (☉ 42)

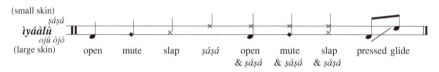

The *omele abo* does not play slap tones, as on the *ìyáàlù* in the previous example but only plays open and mute tones on the *ojú òjò*, as notated in Example i.ii.

Example i.ii.   Notation of the *omele abo* (☉ 42)

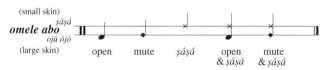

The *omele akọ* and *omele mẹ́ta*, which have two and three skins respectively, are notated with two and three-line percussion staves respectively (listen to ☉ 42, where Àyándòkun plays the three skins of the three small drums).

Example i.iii.   Notation of the *omele akọ* (☉ 42)

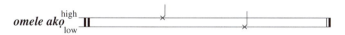

Example i.iv.   Notation of the *omele mẹ́ta* (☉ 42)

The musical examples written in rhythms over a regular pulse and within a metric scheme use conventional rhythmic notation, whereas the examples in free time (direct speech mode) place strokes on the stave spaced approximately as they are rendered in real time. Pauses are marked by an apostrophe above the stave to indicate how Àyándòkun phrased the rendition (see Examples App.II.2–11). Where two strokes are played in rapid succession in free speech mode (as a flam or grace note), they are marked with a slur to highlight their linguistic significance. Fast and slow flams are spaced accordingly. In Example i.v, the fourth flam is faster than the first three. Small note values in metric notation are marked by grace notes or short note values, as illustrated after the double bar line in the same example.

Example i.v.   Notation of small note values and flams

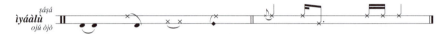

I have notated the rhythms in 'dance time' in 2/2 or 6/8. Notating West African rhythms with Western notation (and therefore superimposing Western concepts) is usually controversial, but I have chosen 2/2 and 6/8 to reflect two underlying beats per bar cycle where the shortest note values are notated with semiquavers. Note values and rests do not represent actual note durations, but are usually chosen for ease of reading. Nevertheless, the longest note value used in my *bàtá* transcriptions is the dotted crotchet, as notes would not normally sustain beyond this due to the *bàtá's* fast-decaying sound.

The *dùndún* transcriptions in Chapter 3 use a three-line stave like that of the *omele mẹ́ta*. This is a gross simplification of what the *dùndún* plays, in order to make a broad comparison with the *bàtá ìyáàlù* and the *omele mẹ́ta*. The *dùndún* actually has a wide pitch range and the three relative pitch tones regularly shift. Unlike Euba (1990), who transcribes the absolute pitches played, along with detailed rhythm transcriptions and the differentiated stick strokes, I have reduced what the *dùndún* plays to a fixed three-line stave and notated the *oríkì* with stemless note heads in free time.

Orthography

The Yorùbá language has eighteen consonants, seven oral vowels and five nasal vowels plus a syllabic nasal. Yorùbá is a true tone language with three relative tone (pitch) bands represented in writing by acute accent marks over high tones, grave accent marks over low tones and no diacritical marks over mid tones. For example:

> high tone – such as *wá* (verb) to come, to search for or to tremble;
> mid tone – such as *wa* (possessive pronoun) our, (object pronoun) us;
> low tone – such as *wà* (verb) to be (in a place), to exist, to dig, to drive, to embrace.

Subdots indicate the following differences:

    e (roughly as in English 'g<u>ay</u>')
    ẹ (roughly as in English 'g<u>et</u>')
    o (roughly as in English 'g<u>o</u>')
    ọ (roughly as in British English 'g<u>o</u>t')
    s (roughly as in English '<u>so</u>')
    ṣ (roughly as in English '<u>sh</u>ow')

The letter *n* represents four distinct effects in Yorùbá:

1. When followed by a vowel, it is pronounced like an English [n].
2. At the end of a word or before a consonant, it nasalizes the preceding vowel (as in French) but is not itself pronounced as a separate sound. Unlike in French, the nasalized vowels otherwise hardly change their pronunciation, though in standard Yorùbá the sequence *an* becomes almost identical in pronunciation to *ọn*, resulting in near-homophones such as Àyàn and Àyọ̀n.
3. As a separate word, the single letter *n* represents a 'syllabic nasal', forming a syllabic nucleus all by itself. One such example is *ń,* which is a continuous marker: *mò ń lọ* [I am (in the act of) going].
4. The nasal consonant *n* also sometimes nasalizes a following word-final vowel, e.g., *inú* 'inside, belly' (which is spelt *inún* in other orthographies, such as Abraham 1958).

Written *p* is pronounced as the voiceless labio-velar stop [kp] where [k] and [p] are simultaneously pronounced, e.g., Ṣọ̀pọ̀nnọ́ (name of an *òrìṣà*). (There is no English [p] in Yorùbá.) In the labio-velar stop *gb*, [g] and [b] are pronounced simultaneously – for example, Òṣogbo (name of a town). Yorùbá also includes English [b], (such as *bàtá)* and English [g], (such as *gúdúgúdú).*

Although the word *àwọn* may precede a noun to denote its plural form, singular and plural nouns are the same. For example, *bàtá* may refer to one or more drums.

Outline of the Chapters

This book offers the most comprehensive description and analysis of the *bàtá's* surrogate speech technology up to the time of writing and, alongside Euba's monumental study (1990), explains in detail how Yorùbá drummers communicate with their drums. My exposition is linear and methodical, so the reader will benefit most from following the narrative and organization of my technical findings as set out in the book. It is recommended that the reader has the CD ready to play while reading the text in order to engage fully with the following chapters, which refer to numerous transcribed and recorded musical examples. (One can, of course, also listen to the CD for the sheer pleasure of it.)

Chapter 1 prepares the reader with historical and contextual information and introduces the Yorùbá people and their drumming, along with the personalities (including my two research collaborators) who offer a narrative about the *bàtá* drum's speech surrogacy technology.

Chapter 2 describes the textual genres of the *bàtá* (*oríkì*, *òwe* and *ìlù òrìṣà*) in more detail and explains how these repertoires are applied practically and contextually by *bàtá* players. I critique Thieme's 1969 study of the *bàtá's* speech surrogacy, which has led to the circulation of misunderstandings about its talking technology. Oyèlámì's 1991 study provides the basis for establishing a grammar for how the *bàtá* talks, while the remainder of the chapter both refines and challenges Oyèlámì's observations in order to build a more detailed model of how the drum encodes speech.

Chapter 3 presents historical and technical information about the *omele mẹta* and the *dùndún* and compares their speech encoding systems both with each other and with the *ìyáàlù bàtá*. In doing so, and illustrating the contrasting techniques of each drum, I begin to deconstruct the idea that the *bàtá* is an inferior speech surrogacy instrument, as is widely believed.

Having laid out how the *bàtá* talks in relation to other Yorùbá drums, Chapter 4 unpacks the fascinating coded spoken language of *alubàtá* by exploring how *ẹnà* utterances relate to *bàtá* drum strokes, how the *ẹnà* syllables derive from spoken Yorùbá and how *ẹnà bàtá* relates to other Yorùbá language codes. The analysis also establishes that some cross-cultural acoustic-phonetic principles are accessed by the *ẹnà* vocable system. The analysis climaxes with a theoretical model of a Yorùbá-*ẹnà*-*bàtá* cycle, which resembles models applied in information science to creating machine language.

The Epilogue explains the inter-related areas of performer, instrument and listener and, in doing so, locates points of possible communication breakdown in order to absolve the *bàtá* of its reputation as a 'poor talker'. Rather, this final chapter leaves the reader with an understanding of the *bàtá's* – and of course the *alubàtá's* – amazing sophistication in transmitting detailed semantic messages with knowledge, wood and leather.

How (Not) to Use this Book

This volume is not a how-to-play-*bàtá* instruction manual. Rather, it is an analysis of the drummed speech surrogacy system and *ẹnà bàtá*, the coded spoken language of *bàtá* drummers. Rather than functioning as a set of prescriptive materials, the recordings, transcriptions and explanations presented within are examples that serve the analysis. Although the recordings and transcriptions can give musicians an insight into how to play the *bàtá*, they are best employed as a preparation for studying with a master drummer such as Rábíù Àyándòkun.

Ultimately, my research collaborators and I want the reader to share our wonder, fascination and respect for the Yorùbá *bàtá* and its ancient text messages.

Chapter 1
The Telegraph without Wire

On my first day in Rábíù Àyándòkun's compound in Ẹ̀rìn-Ọ̀ṣun, he interrupted our conversation by picking up a *bàtá* drum and playing something that – to my perception at the time – sounded like a free-time improvization. When a young man burst into the room about ten minutes later, out of breath and holding another *bàtá* drum, Àyándòkun giggled proudly, telling me that he had drummed a message to the young man, asking him to bring the drum from a neighbouring compound. Àyándòkun was aware that I had come to Nigeria to research the *bàtá* drum language and he knew that he would impress me with this demonstration of distance communication, which I am told can stretch up to two kilometres on a quiet day in the town. Over the following years, I witnessed various kinds of drum communications (not always for my benefit) during my fieldwork in Ẹ̀rìn-Ọ̀ṣun. My desire to understand the *bàtá's* communication system has escalated over the past decade and has culminated in this volume.

When I first visited Ẹ̀rìn-Ọ̀ṣun in September 1999, the town took forty-five minutes to an hour to reach on a very rough gravel road from the nearest large town, Òṣogbo – if one could find a taxi driver who was willing to make the journey. If it was raining, there was almost no chance of convincing a driver to go there. The town's relative isolation was not just due to the poor road, which the king of Ẹ̀rìn-Ọ̀ṣun has since negotiated with local government to replace with a wide paved road. Before 2002, Ẹ̀rìn-Ọ̀ṣun also had never had telephones. Despite its isolation, Ẹ̀rìn-Ọ̀ṣun has long been well known throughout Nigeria for its compounds of Yorùbá Àyàn (born) drummers who use their drums to transmit what I have paradoxically labelled 'ancient text messages', an expression that captures the encounter of old and new technologies. While nobody knows just how old the *bàtá* drum's surrogate speech technology actually is, it is 'ancient' in the Àyàn drummer imaginary, and certainly much older than the 'text messages' rendered by mobile telephones and emails.

Following a global telecommunications revolution, people in remote and underdeveloped regions of the world now communicate with low-cost text messages transmitted by mobile telephones. While most of the world was using mobile telephones by 2000, including the majority of countries in sub-Saharan Africa, nearly all of Nigeria was still limping along with the notoriously unreliable government landline telephone network called Nigerian Telecommunications Limited, popularly known as NITEL. It was out of the financial reach of many poor Nigerians to install a NITEL line, and smaller communities and outposts such as Ẹ̀rìn-Ọ̀ṣun were never included in government road, health and communication infrastructures. (Up until late 2007, Àyándòkun had to drive to Òṣogbo every day to check his emails.) The mobile phone revolution belatedly started in Nigeria in 2001 with the instigation of

GSM telephone networks across the country. GSM transmission masts were first installed in the largest urban and financial centres, but when I visited Ẹ̀rìn-Ọ̀ṣun in April 2002, my mobile still could not receive a signal there. The people of Ẹ̀rìn-Ọ̀ṣun finally got connected to a national telephone network – for the first time ever – in late 2002. One wonders how the widespread use of telephones will impact on Ẹ̀rìn-Ọ̀ṣun's drummed ancient text message technology, as the *bàtá* is already an endangered tradition in a fast modernizing society.

On that same 1999 trip, I also heard for the first time the spoken coded language of *bàtá* drummers, which they call *ẹnà*.[1] This coded language immediately became another source of fascination for me, although initially I had no knowledge of how *ẹnà* was interconnected with *bàtá* drumming techniques, and how understanding the rudimentary mapping rules of *ẹnà* would provide data for the *bàtá's* speech surrogacy system. Remarkably, *alubàtá* (*bàtá* drummers) are the only Yorùbá drummers to speak a specific coded language. Therefore, *ẹnà* too qualifies as 'ancient text messages' in an environment where Yorùbá people have been educated in English since colonialism and are conditioned to believe that speaking English well brings social and economic ascendancy. Contemporary Yorùbá people are bombarded by English-speaking media and hence use more and more English loan words in modern Yorùbá vernaculars. *Ẹnà*, which relies on knowledge of *ìjìnlẹ̀* Yorùbá (deep Yorùbá) is a receding indigenous communication technology within a fast-changing culture.

The *bàtá* drumming tradition is around five hundred years old and is associated with the *òrìṣà* (spiritual being) Ṣàngó, who is the deified fifteenth-century king of the town of Ọ̀yọ́. The *bàtá* is still strongly associated with Ọ̀yọ́ and the Ṣàngó cult, although it also has wider religious associations, including other *òrìṣà* cults such as Èṣù, the divine messenger, Ọya, Ṣàngó's mythological queen and Egúngún, the *òrìṣà* of ancestors. Mythological sources suggest that the *bàtá* originated among the Nupe people north of the Niger River and diffused south to what is now known as Yorùbáland, where it was institutionalized and popularized in the old Ọ̀yọ́ kingdom[2] around the fourteenth and fifteenth centuries. As the Ọ̀yọ́ kingdom expanded its political and cultural influence (peaking in the eighteenth century), the *bàtá* tradition diffused outward from Ọ̀yọ́ and can now be found all over Yorùbáland, including areas of the Republic of Bénin to the west. The further *bàtá* traditions are from the current Ọ̀yọ́ geographically, the more diverse the traditions are. For example, Ìjẹbú, in southern Yorùbáland, and Kétu, in the west, have quite distinct *bàtá* traditions from that of contemporary Ọ̀yọ́, which

---

[1]   The term *ẹnà* can be applied generically to encompass different language coding systems. Although there are different kinds of *ẹnà* (see Ìṣọ̀lá 1982), I use the term throughout this text in specific reference to *ẹnà bàtá*.

[2]   Ọ̀yọ́ Ilé ('old Ọ̀yọ́') was located further north (above the rainforest region and south of the Niger River) than the current Ọ̀yọ́, which was established in the 1830s at which time Ọ̀yọ́ Ilé was abandoned due to civil wars and the *jihad* approaching from the north. See Law 1997 and Smith 1988.

is the style of the current study. Across the Atlantic, the *batá* tradition in Cuba, which evolved through the transatlantic slave trade, is popular and thriving.[3] The expression 'the telegraph without wire' was coined by one of Cuba's late *batá* masters and religious elders, Estéban 'Cha Chá' Vega. Vega used the phrase to capture this drum's capacity to transcend time and space and communicate with both humans and spirits close by and afar.[4]

Secret or Little-known?

Although the *bàtá* developed an intentionally obscure system of encoding Yorùbá speech in past times in order to communicate exclusively with ritual insiders (*awo*), the collection of data and the publication of the drum's coding processes in this book present no ethical problems. While the *bàtá* once functioned exclusively as a cult and war drum within the Ọ̀yọ́ empire and communicated messages exclusively to *awo*, the drum's talking technology and its textual material necessarily excluded ritual outsiders (*ọ̀gbẹ̀rì*). The methods developed to transform ordinary Yorùbá speech into a spoken code, and then into a coded drum language, once served the needs of cult secrecy. However, the social function of the *bàtá* drum has transformed dramatically over the past century.

Most Yorùbá people are now Muslim or Christian (said to be fifty per cent and forty-five per cent respectively) and the overwhelming majority of inherited Àyàn drummers (which include *alubàtá*) are Muslims. As the traditional *òrìṣà* ritual practices continue to recede due to modernization and Muslim and Christian conversion, *alubàtá* serve a dwindling *òrìṣà* community in contemporary Nigeria. Hence, the *bàtá* is slowly (and at times contentiously) creeping into secular realms, where it is used more to provide dance rhythms than for the transmission of semantic messages. Yet as the knowledge of sacred drum texts and the coded language, *ẹ̀nà bàtá*, diminishes among *alubàtá*, the whole tradition of the Yorùbá *bàtá* as a talking drum is endangered. Àyándòkun has repeatedly articulated his anxiety that Àyàn lineage knowledge of the *bàtá*'s encoding method, texts and musical repertoire will be permanently lost, stating, for example, 'We don't want to forget. Now if I don't work this out, it is going to be lost. Not many people know now' (personal communication, London, 31 March 2007).

While I commenced my own research on the *bàtá* drum language in the mid 1990s, I am neither the first nor the only agent involved in the project of 'cracking the code'. Múráínà Oyèlámì launched his study of the *bàtá*'s drum language as

---

[3]   The accent in the Cuban spelling, *batá*, represents stress rather than relative speech tone as in Yorùbá.

[4]   Vega was also known as a *rumba* musician (*rumbero*) and founding member of the state-funded ensemble *Los Muñequitos de Matanzas*. *Rumberos* use the expression *telegrafo antiquo* [old telegraph] to describe the 'talking' of the lead drum, the *quinto*, in the *rumba* ensemble. However, the *quinto* does not actually encode speech.

much as a decade earlier, publishing his findings in 1991. Oyèlámì was preceded by Akin Euba who published research on the *dùndún's* drum language (1975, 1990). As early as 1982, Ìṣọlá published on *ẹnà* (Yorùbá coded languages). All three scholars have co-operated in my research at different points, as have some thirty Yorùbá drummers. While some of the esoteric knowledge of initiations and drum consecrations is deemed secret, the drum language is regarded differently. Drummers were invariably happy to teach me drummed texts, and all knew I was working towards publication.

Although *ẹnà bàtá* evolved as a communication system to exclude people outside of *bàtá* lineages, its contemporary use is transforming as it contracts. As I explain in Chapter 4, not only is *ẹnà bàtá* now incorporating other Yorùbá code systems, but knowledge of the language is also endangered. Like the *bàtá* speech surrogacy system, *ẹnà bàtá* is little-known, as opposed to secret. Accordingly, Àyándòkun and other *bàtá* drummers have co-operated with my study. Echoing my own field experience, my research collaborator Adégbọlá declared:

> The attitude of members of the Àyàn lineage suggests that the obscurity of *ẹnà bàtá* derives more from the complexity of the system than a desire for secrecy among the Àyàn. Even though members of the Àyàn lineage celebrate the exclusivity of the knowledge of *ẹnà bàtá*, my experience was more of marvel than indignation when I flaunted my limited *ẹnà bàtá* vocabulary to Àyánújí Àmọó, a celebrated Lagos-based drummer from Òṣogbo. He only lamented his own receding vocabulary (personal communication, email, 6 December 2007).

While Àyándòkun has always been enthusiastic about documenting the *bàtá* tradition, the aspect of the research that he embraced most enthusiastically was the recording process. In Àyándòkun's view, recordings are an extremely important resource for future preservation and transmission. While most of his sons and nephews show limited interest in concentrated study of the drum, Àyándòkun envisages a time when the recordings we made can be a learning resource for young Àyàn drummers in his family after the elders have died.

Overall, Àyándòkun's attitude towards research and publication is pragmatic. In regard of the *bàtá* language's obscurity, he stated, 'When researchers have an interest to learn about the *bàtá*, I have to tell them what they want to know. Otherwise this thing is dead' (personal communication, London, June 2005).

The Articulate 'Stammerer'

It is the relative obscurity of the *bàtá's* speech surrogacy system – and even its efficiency as a code – that may have contributed to its erroneous reputation as a poor communication instrument compared to the less obscure *dùndún*. Far from being widely recognized as having developed one of the most refined communicative systems in Yorùbá drumming, and perhaps even West African drumming, the *bàtá* has an unfortunate reputation as a 'stammerer'. In this volume I present evidence that debunks this negative label and explains how the *bàtá* is at least as good a talker as the more popular *dùndún* drum, which uses a different, yet overlapping, speech surrogate system.

When I first began researching the *bàtá's* speech surrogacy some ten years ago, the drum's reputation as an inferior talker was not corroborated by my data, which uncovered a remarkable range of techniques to represent Yorùbá human speech. It was not until I had an informal conversation with linguist 'Túndé Adégbọlá in January 2004 that I learned that the Yorùbá word *kólòlò* – a verb-noun elision of *kó òlòlò*, which is frequently used to describe what the *bàtá* does – is usually translated into English as 'to stammer'. Adégbọlá drew my attention to the fact that an alternative translation of *kólòlò* is 'to speak in a *staccato* (short and detached) manner'. The noun *òlòlò* is usually translated as 'stammer', while *akólòlò* is a noun usually translated as 'the one who stammers'. If one considers the alternative meanings of *kólòlò* as 'speak in a *staccato* manner', *òlòlò* as 'short detached utterance' and *akólòlò* as 'one who speaks in a *staccato* manner' (each of which I have corroborated with linguist Akin Oyètádé), a new set of possibilities emerges. If one 'stammers', he speaks with halting articulation with pauses or rapid repetitions of the same syllable, perhaps temporarily due to nervousness, or habitually due to a speech impediment. The *bàtá* does in fact rapidly repeat syllables from time to time for aesthetic and rhythmic reasons as several of the transcriptions in this volume exemplify, but so does the *dùndún*, creating what Euba (1990:230–235) labels 'false syllables'. Yet Euba (or anyone else, to my knowledge) does not label the *dùndún* a 'stammerer' for this stylistic feature, which strengthens my assertion that '*kólòlò*' refers to a speech dimension other than syllable repetition. Adégbọlá's reinterpretations of the relevant Yorùbá words opens up an alternative understanding: the verb *kólòlò* indicates that the *bàtá* speaks fluently in its characteristic punctuated, short and detached manner. It does not stammer.

Unlike the *dùndún*, which produces relatively sustained notes (and therefore is able to emulate the *glissandi* of Yorùbá speech with its variable pitch technique), the *bàtá's* notes decay quickly, resulting in stabbing, punctuated sounds with a high transient at the front of the sound. Applying European musical terminology, while the *bàtá* is *staccato*, the *dùndún* is *staccato's* opposite, *legato* (connected smoothly). (Compare ☉ 9 and ☉ 34). The *bàtá's* lack of sustain requires alternative techniques for mimicking speech glides, which I illustrate in Chapter 2.

The *bàtá's* reputation as an inferior talker was probably first implied in 1954 when ethnographer Beier (who is neither a musician nor music scholar) made a comparison between the *dùndún* and the *bàtá*: 'It is much more difficult to talk on it [the *bàtá*], and far more difficult to understand it' (1954:30). The probable English mistranslation of the words *kólòlò/akólòlò* and the *bàtá's* subsequent reputation as a stammerer first appeared in an article by one of Beier's informants, cultural authority and drumming patron Láoyè I, Tìmì (king) of Ẹdẹ, who stated, 'The Iya Ilu [lead] Bata though suited for talking does so with some difficulty being a stammerer' (1959:10).[5] In a later article, Láoyè adds, 'It [the *bàtá*] is even reputed for its talkativeness which is characteristic of stammerers' (1966:38). In a lecture demonstration (mostly in English) at Ìbàdàn University in 1966,[6] Láoyè further reiterated the *dùndún's* semantic superiority, saying, 'The *bàtá*, although a stammerer, can also talk elaborately, for people to understand. And it can be used to transmit messages, also. But the drum that is used for talking and which is most elaborate in trying to imitate human tone is the *dùndún*.' Yet it is interesting that Láoyè states that the *bàtá* can nevertheless 'talk elaborately', which may support my conjecture that he had translated *kólòlò* and *akólòlò* narrowly.[7] While also upholding the idea that the *dùndún* is a superior talker, Omíbíyìí (1978:480) is marginally more cautious in stating, 'The tension drum [*dùndún*] is better equipped for talking than any other type of Yorùbá drum and it is a point of conjecture whether or not the *bàtá* is more talkative than even the *ìyáàlù* of the *dùndún* orchestra'.

Although I vigorously challenge the notion that the *bàtá* has difficulty talking (that is, representing speech), there is, in fact, truth in each of the above statements. *Bàtá* players are proud of the fact that their instrument is technically more difficult to learn and play than the *dùndún* and other Yorùbá drums, and they invariably say that the *bàtá* requires a longer apprenticeship, which is undoubtedly part of the reason that *dùndún* players are now much more common than *alubàtá* (*bàtá* players). It is also indisputable that the *bàtá* is more difficult to understand for most Yorùbá speakers than the *dùndún*. Firstly, this is partly due to the *dùndún*'s large pitch range and gliding capacity, which make it more aurally accessible to Yorùbá speakers. The *bàtá*, with its narrower range of pitch variation, has a different technique of representing tone glides and is less accessible to listeners unfamiliar with its mode of speech. As tone carries a high lexical load in the Yorùbá language, listeners rely on relative pitch and *glissandi* above and beyond other parameters of speech when interpreting the messages of the *dùndún*.

Secondly, the *bàtá's* problem of intelligibility amongst contemporary Yorùbá people is largely due to the fact that it is more contextually restricted than the *dùndún*. As the *bàtá* is inextricably linked with the pre-Christian and Muslim traditional religion, *òrìṣà* devotion, and has not been widely appropriated by the church or passed into secular use and popular music as the *dùndún* has, Yorùbá listeners are less familiar with the way the *bàtá* represents speech. As it is a religious drum, *bàtá* texts are often idiomatic and demand background knowledge

---

[5]   Although Láoyè wrote in English and I have no concrete evidence that his use of the word 'stammerer' is a mistranslation of *akólòlò*, my collaborator Adégbọlá suggested a mistranslation based on the common employment of the words *kólòlò* and *akólòlò* in relationship to the *bàtá*.

[6]   This lecture was recorded by Doig Simmonds, who kindly forwarded the recording to me in December 2007.

[7]   Despite the controversy over the words *kólòlò/akólòlò*, Adégbọlá assessed Láoyè's translations of *òwe* and other drum texts in the lecture as extraordinarily good.

of sacred texts. (Indeed, unpacking any musical surrogate speech system requires contextual knowledge.)

Thirdly, as the *bàtá* was and is an instrument of a mystical tradition and early sources also tell us that it was a war drum, its cryptic nature was probably intentional in order to transmit messages only to 'those in the know'. My paradoxical thesis is that the *bàtá* is less immediately intelligible than the *dùndún* due to its essentially different function. Provocatively, I propose that the *bàtá's* relative unintelligibility is due to the limitations of contemporary Yorùbá listeners rather than any technical limitations of the instrument or its speaking technology or indeed its drummers.

Previous Studies of Speech Surrogacy and Yorùbá Drumming

There is a substantial body of work, spanning the twentieth century, about other (non-Yorùbá) African speech surrogacy systems, including Rattray (1923), Stern (1957), Cooke (1970), Sebeok (1976), Nketia (1976, 2002), Carrington (1976), Locke and Agbeli (1980) and Agawu (1995:31–60). There are numerous texts about Yorùbá drumming generally (e.g., Láoyè 1959, 1966 and Thieme 1969), while some touch on the speech surrogacy of Yorùbá drums (Beier 1954, Euba 1975 & 1990, Bankole *et al.* 1975, Omíbíyìí 1978 and Àjàyí 1990) and some address *bàtá* drum language specifically (Beier, Láoyè, Bankole *et al*, Omíbíyìí, Thieme and Euba). The little that has been written about the Nigerian *bàtá* has also focused primarily on the Ọ̀yọ́ style (Bascom 1953, Thieme 1969, Oyèlámì 1991, D. Klein 2000, Marcuzzi 2005) and styles in The People's Republic of Bénin (Rouget 1965, Branda-Lacerda 1988). Only Thieme and Klein touch on the *bàtá's* speech surrogacy. Although he is not a scholar, Oyèlámì (1991) produced a very important and innovative text, without which my own work may possibly have not evolved in the way it has. Euba's studies of the *dùndún* (1975, 1990) have also been crucial in developing my research, and indeed I draw upon Euba's research rather than conducting concentrated *dùndún* research myself.

I have only been able to locate one text about *ẹnà*; Ìṣọ̀lá (1982), which is a generic study but does not refer to the *ẹnà* of *bàtá* drummers at all. One of my research collaborators, Marcuzzi, presented a conference paper (2004) using *ẹnà* data I collected and made available to him, while two Hughes articles (1989, 2000) contributed significantly to our thinking about *ẹnà*. This volume therefore presents the first published research about *ẹnà*, which makes a significant contribution to what is known about the *bàtá* drum language.

Not only does this volume offer the first comprehensive body of information about how the *bàtá* drum's speech surrogacy technology functions, it is also the first serious comparison of the *bàtá* and the *dùndún*, based on hard data rather than cultural opinion. Beyond the specifics of Yorùbá drumming, this volume also constitutes one of the most detailed studies of an African speech surrogacy form.

The Yorùbá People and their Religious Practices

The people now known as 'the Yorùbá' in southwest Nigeria and southeast Republic of Bénin were once a geographically spread set of loosely connected ethnic groups who spoke mutually intelligible regional dialects, including the Òyó in the central region, the Kétu and Ègbádò to the west of Òyó, the Ègbá, Ìjèbú and Òwu to the south, and the Oǹdó and Èkìtì to the east. These peoples (and perhaps another twenty such sub-groups) still speak differentiated dialects of what is now called 'Yorùbá language' and self-identify as Yorùbá people.

The actual word 'Yorùbá' originally derived from the Hausa/Arabic terms *Yariba, Yarriba, Yarraba, Yarba, Yarub, Yarabawa* or *Yaruba,* and was applied by the Hausa in the north of Nigeria up until the nineteenth century, specifically to designate their southern neighbours, the Òyó people. (See Waterman 1990a, Law 1997 and Peel 2000:283–88 for fuller accounts of how Yorùbá identity developed.) As Òyó became a powerful empire in the seventeenth century and conquered many surrounding regions, the term Yorùbá was increasingly used to include the peoples under Òyó control. By the second half of the nineteenth century, missionaries expanded the term yet again to represent 'the "neo-Yorùbá" nation of the Christian imaginary' (Peel 2000), including other neighbouring groups speaking mutually intelligible dialects and returnees[8] from Sierra Leone (the Aku, Saro and Amaro). Because of this nineteenth-century double usage of 'Yorùbá' as both a marker of the Òyó people and as a generic term for their neighbouring peoples and returnees, the Òyó became distinguished as the 'Yorùbá proper'. It was not until the late nineteenth century that Yorùbá became a generic term for the large ethnic group it designates today.

As there were no 'Yorùbá', as we know it today, until just over a century ago, there was therefore no generic 'Yorùbá religion'. Rather, prior to the missionary activity in Yorùbáland which began around the 1840s, there were regional, loosely connected cults. Of this period, Peel (2000:121) states, 'So the "traditional religion" of the Yorùbá does not really present itself as a single, given, separate entity. What it designates concretely is a congeries of cultic practices, actuated by some common principles, but varying a great deal over space and over time.' As peoples of the region coalesced into a larger ethnic identity, their variegated regional spiritual practices became increasingly identified with a single religious system, now broadly known as 'Òrìṣà Religion' or 'Òrìṣà Tradition'.[9] It is difficult to say exactly how far back in time any of the *òrìṣà* cults reach, but their ritual practices may well date back to before 1000AD. They certainly pre-date, by

---

[8] 'Returnees' refers to those people on slave ships leaving from West Africa that were interrupted by British patrols after the British abolition of slavery (1807). Large numbers of the rescued captives, who were repatriated in Sierra Leone, returned to Nigeria.

[9] Palmié (2007:160) questions the appropriateness of the post-Reformation western category of 'religion' to characterize 'whatever is going on' in terms of ritual practices in Africa.

several centuries, the introduction of Islam (since the late sixteenth century) and Christianity (since the 1840s).

Since the 1950s, an increasingly monotheistic representation of *Òrìṣà* tradition has been promoted and systematized by Yorùbá Christian scholars such as Lucas, Awolalu and Ìdòwú, who have endeavoured to represent *Òrìṣà* Tradition as a *bona fide* religion analogous to Islam and Christianity. These and other Christian scholars formalized the *òrìṣà* into an organized 'pantheon' or 'cosmology' with a God Almighty at the head, known as Olódùmarè or Ọlọrun. The notion of a 'Yorùbá pantheon' has been reproduced by many foreign scholars (for examples, see Drewal and Pemberton 1989:14 and Drewal & J. Mason 1998:20 for formulaic diagrams of the *òrìṣà* 'pantheon'). However, Church Missionary Society data presented by Peel (2000:117) challenges the model of an Almighty God and a 'ministry' (Ìdòwú 1994:57–106) of lesser beings (*òrìṣà*) by demonstrating that nineteenth-century devotees often understood their own *òrìṣà* to be the creator or God the Supreme Being (not Olódùmarè or Ọlọrun, as many twentieth-century scholars and devotees claim). Whatever the history of the contemporary model of God Almighty (Olódùmarè/Ọlọrun) with a subsidiary *òrìṣà* pantheon, this paradigm appears to have been internalized by contemporary Yorùbá devotees and the enormous Yorùbá religious diaspora in Cuba, Brazil, Trinidad and beyond.

The Yorùbá word *òrìṣà* does not have a reliable translation, although it is often translated into English as 'gods', 'deities' or 'fetishes'. Devotees (who usually refer to themselves in English as 'devotees' or 'traditionalists'[10]) believe that *òrìṣà* are all-knowing, omnipresent spiritual beings with access to the past, present and future. Devotees believe that *òrìṣà* have the power to intercept physical reality and facilitate healing, conception and birth, material wealth and other blessings. Conversely, they are also believed to have a potential destructive power. Hence it is important to petition and appease the *òrìṣà* through prayer, praise, music and sacrificial offerings. Accordingly, *òrìṣà* devotees need to pray regularly, to give sacrificial offerings, and to receive, study and perform divination. Devotees must also spend time learning the oral literature, invocatory repertoire, song texts and ritual gestures in order to be ritually and socially effective. The *òrìṣà* are believed to communicate with humans through spirit possession, divination, dreams, visions and other visitations. Prayers, songs, other oral incantations and drumming, which often encodes spoken incantations, are considered to be important methods of communication for devotees to communicate with the *òrìṣà*.

It is often said – both in the literature and by devotees – that there are 401 *òrìṣà*, although this is a metaphoric number to represent the vast and dynamic cohort of *òrìṣà* throughout Yorùbáland. In this volume, I present drum rhythms (*ìlù òrìṣà*) and a form of oral literature called *oríkì* (described below). I recorded fifteen *ìlù òrìṣà* rhythms, and sixteen *oríkì òrìṣà*, chosen by Àyándòkun and me according to what repertoire is most common in his area and therefore is most

---

[10]   'Traditionalist', as a term in opposition to 'Christian' or 'Muslim', has probably only been in use in Nigeria since the 1960s.

familiar to him. The material presented in the transcriptions and recordings in this volume are samples of different corpuses but are not corpuses in themselves. They are randomly ordered, according to the examples illustrating the text, but do not reflect the way the material is ordered and performed *in situ*.

In order to give some context to *ìlù òrìṣà* and *oríkì òrìṣà* presented to the reader, the following will help contextualize the texts. Some *òrìṣà* are considered to be deified mythological historical personalities. For example Ṣàngó was the mythological fifteenth-century king of Ọ̀yọ́. Ọya, a warrior queen, was one of Ṣàngó's wives and is believed to be of Nupe origin (north of the Yorùbá). Another of Ṣàngó's wives was Ọ̀ṣun, who was also a warrior queen and the mythological originator of the town of Òṣogbo. She is said to have halted the *jihad* descending from the north. Other *òrìṣà* are considered never to have taken human form (for example, Orí, the *òrìṣà* of personal destiny).

Many *òrìṣà* are understood to embody forces of nature (for example, Ṣàngó is also known as the *òrìṣà* of thunder and lightning; Ọya is the *òrìṣà* of tornados; Ọ̀ṣun, Yemọja and Ọ̀tìn are river *òrìṣà* and Òrìṣà Òkè is represented by a large rock formation). Other *òrìṣà* cults are integral to social organization and are tied in with family craft lineages (for example, Ògún is the *òrìṣà* of blacksmiths and hunters; Ọ̀ṣọ́ọ̀sì is also an *òrìṣà* of hunters; Ọ̀tìn, her husband Ọbẹ̀dú and Erinlẹ̀ are also mythological hunters; Òrìṣà Oko is the *òrìṣà* of farming; while Ọbàlùfọ̀n is the *òrìṣà* of cloth and weaving). Some *òrìṣà* represent human archetypes, such as Yemọja, who is the supreme mother; Ọ̀ṣun, who represents femininity, sexuality and fertility; Ìbejì, who is the *òrìṣà* of twins; and Ọbàtálá, who is the wise old man on the mountain and the *òrìṣà* of creativity who helped created the earth and presides over the formation of foetuses in the womb.

Many of the cults have their own medicinal technologies, such as Ṣọ̀pọ̀nnọ́, the *òrìṣà* of smallpox, whose priests knew the secret of vaccination at least a century before Western Europe (personal communication, Adégbọlá). Likewise, the Ifá cult, which worships the *òrìṣà* of divination, Ọ̀rúnmìlà, has a cohort of priests (*babaláwo*) known for their powerful medicine. Women with fertility problems most usually go to see Ọ̀ṣun or Yemọja priests who are renowned for their fertility remedies.

The *òrìṣà* were predominately regional in pre-colonial times. For example, Ọ̀ṣun was the founder of Òṣogbo; Ṣàngó was the founder of Ọ̀yọ́; Yemọja was concentrated in Abẹ́òkúta; Òrìṣà Òkè originated in rocky Ìrágbìjí; Ọbẹ̀dú was centred in Ọbà; Ọ̀tìn and Erinlẹ̀ are said to have lived in the river in Ìlóbùú; and Ọbàlùfọ̀n and Ifá originated in Ilé-Ifẹ̀, the mythological 'cradle of Yorùbá civilization'. Other *òrìṣà* such as Èṣù, Ìbejì and Ọbàtálá are much more widely distributed. While certain towns such as those named above are considered to be centres of origin and devotion for specific *òrìṣà*, most *òrìṣà* are now widely geographically distributed. One sees frequent references to the *òrìṣà's* towns of origin in the drum texts and *oríkì*.

There are several *òrìṣà* that are particularly important to *bàtá* drummers. The most important is Àyàn, who is both the mythological, deified progenitor of drumming and the *òrìṣà* of Yorùbá drumming craft lineages. Although the *bàtá* play for almost all *òrìṣà* (although there are little-known *òrìṣà* in areas where *bàtá* is not common), these drums have a particularly close relationship with Ṣàngó, who is said to 'own' the *bàtá* and was mythologically involved with their popularization during his reign. The *bàtá* is also Ọya's drum and the closely related Egúngún, which is the *òrìṣà* of the ancestors. The *bàtá* also have a privileged relationship with the very important *òrìṣà* Èṣù, who is the divine messenger between the celestial sphere (*ọ̀run*) and earth (*ayé*).

Yorùbá Drums

Although the Yorùbá people have a wide range of musical instruments (including aerophones and chordophones) and performance practices, their musical culture is best known for drumming (membranophones and idiophones). Most *òrìṣà* cults have their own associated forms of drumming. While the *bàtá* is most closely associated with Ṣàngó, Egúngún, Èṣù and Ọya (although it plays for all *òrìṣà*), there are other dedicated cult ensembles, such as the *àgẹ̀rẹ̀* ensemble for Ògún, *ìgbìn* drums for Ọbàtálá, *àràn* and *ìpèsè* drums for Ifá, *bẹ̀mbẹ́* drums for Ọ̀sun, and *gbẹ̀du* drums, which are used for kingships and the Ògbóni society (the earth cult of jural authority). There are also many drums that have been appropriated or adapted for popular music, such as the *dùndún*, *samba* and *àkúbà*.

Most sacred Yorùbá drums are used as instruments of speech surrogacy, although none are as highly developed as the *dùndún* and the *bàtá*. Next to the *dùndún*, the *bàtá* is by far the most common and widely distributed Yorùbá drum, and is particularly important as the tradition was taken to Cuba via the transatlantic slave trade, where there is now a parallel *bàtá* tradition (spelt *batá* in Cuba). (See Vincent 2006 for a comprehensive comparison of the parallel traditions.) Indeed, the Cuban *batá* has become a symbol of diasporic Yorùbá ethnic identity in Cuba itself, and of the Cuban diaspora in Latin and North America. Due to the wide distribution of the *bàtá*, many non-Nigerians who have an interest in the Nigerian *bàtá* first encountered it through the diasporic *batá* tradition.

Most texts (for example, Láoyè 1959, Thieme 1969, Thompson 1993, Abímbọlá 1997 & 2000) describe the *bàtá* ensemble as being comprised of four or more drums, although my research generally, and most particularly that based on information collected from Àyándòkun and Oyèlámì, asserts that the *bàtá* ensemble is traditionally comprised of three drums and drummers, to which other drums can be added.[11] The largest and leading drum is the *ìyáàlù* (literally 'mother drum'), which is the primary talker, and can do so on its own. (See Illustration 1.1.) The

---

[11]   Despite Àyándòkun's and Oyèlámì's assertions, I have located some ethnographic film from 1928 showing a *bàtá* ensemble of five drummers in Ògbómọ̀ṣọ́. It is difficult to assess whether ensemble sizes varied regionally, and in what time period larger ensembles became more common. The film is *Native Life in West Africa*, c. 1928, catalogue 90.21.1 c. 192, and is in the Human Archives of Human Studies, The Smithsonian Institution.

second drum, the *omele abo* (literally 'female accompanying drum') functions partly as a rhythm-keeper but can also join in when the *ìyáàlù* talks. However, it cannot speak on its own and can only play a supportive speaking role. The *omele akọ* (literally 'male accompanying drum') is a rhythm instrument and does not mimic speech. The term *omele akọ* can refer to a single small drum, or it can be tied to a *kúdi* (as in Illustration 1.1), which has its pitch lowered by a dark tuning paste called *ìda* that is placed in the middle of the skin. Àyándòkun says that the only distinguishing feature between the *omele abo* and the *kúdi* is the placement of *ìda* on the *kúdi*. Once they are tied together, the *kúdi* loses its separate identity; the pair is also known as *omele akọ* and is played by one drummer.

The larger skins of the *ìyáàlù* and the *omele abo* are known as *ojú òjò*[12] and are played with the right hand in Àyándòkun's *bàtá* tradition. The smaller skins of the *ìyáàlù* and the *omele abo* and the larger skins of *omele akọ* (the smaller skins facing the ground are not played) are all called *ṣáṣá* (an onomatopoeic term) and are played with flexible rawhide beaters called *bílálà* (see Illustration 1.2). The brass bells attached to the *ìyáàlù* are called *ṣaworo* or *iṣaworo*, while the straps that suspend the drums around the shoulders of the *alubàtá* are referred to as *apá*. The *ìyáàlù* and *omele abo* are played horizontally, while the *omele akọ* is hung around the shoulders with the *ṣáṣá* facing upward, and is played by the two hands, each holding a *bílálà*.

Only over the past two decades has the *bàtá* gradually moved into more secular use and popular music. In social settings, the *bàtá* is likely to play dance rhythms, often as part of an extended ensemble, which may include the *àdàmọ̀* (a conical, two-headed drum of similar construction to the *omele abo* but played in the upright position with the *bílálà*), the *àkúbà* (a pair of standing or portative drums inspired by Cuban congas) and the *omele méta*, which is similar to the *omele akọ* in Illustration 1.1, but with three drums tied together. (See Illustration 3.1)

The *Bàtá's* Repertoire

Although the *bàtá* is particularly closely associated with the Ṣàngó, Èṣù, Egúngún and Ọya cults, it is frequently used in other *òrìṣà* cults, secular contexts and the

---

[12] Only one of my Yorùbá research participants has been able to explain the significance or etymology of the term *ojú òjò*, which, interpreted literally, could be 'face of rain'. Adégbọlá suggests that as *jò* means 'to leak', *ojú òjò* could be understood as 'the face which leaks'. For example, in colloquial Yorùbá, a person who drinks a lot is sometimes nick-named '*òjò*' (a euphemism for a person who causes beer bottles to leak). Using a similar euphemistic logic, the *ojú òjò* could refer to a face that leaks or talks a lot. The Cubans call this same skin of their *bàtá* the *enú* (from Yorùbá *ẹnu* meaning 'mouth') or in Spanish *la boca*, also 'the mouth'. The Cuban term tends to corroborate the idea that *ojú òjò* is a face that talks a lot.

Illustration 1.1.   The *bàtá* ensemble (from left) – *ìyáàlù, omele abo, omele akọ*

Note: These drums (owned by Hamish Orr) were made by Làmídì Àyánkúnlé. *Ìyáàlù* length 75.5cm; *ojú òjò* (larger skin) diameter 24.5cm; *ṣáṣá* (smaller skin) diameter 13.5cm. *Omele abo* length 53cm; *ojú òjò* diameter 21.5cm; *ṣáṣá* diameter 12cm. *Omele akọ* (left) length 25cm; *ṣáṣá* diameter 11cm. *Omele akọ* (right) length 23cm; *ṣáṣá* diameter 11cm.

Illustration 1.2.   *Bílálà*

Note: These *bílálà* (owned by the author). were made by Rábíù Àyándòkun. The longer *bílálà* (top) is 32cm in length and 2cm at the widest point. The shorter *bílálà* is 26cm in length and 3cm at the widest point. (The longer *bílálà* are generally used on the *omele akọ* and *omele méta*, while the shorter one is used for the *ìyáàlù* and *omele abo ṣáṣá*.)

church (although the latter is still quite rare). In its cult use, the *bàtá* has a mostly instrumental repertoire. One rarely hears singers with this repertoire, although at times one can hear dancers and devotees (but never the drummers) chant along with drum texts they recognize in instrumental repertoires. One might also hear a simultaneous performance of oral literature alongside the *bàtá* rhythms, but the *bàtá* does not accompany the vocal performers, as it is not providing the rhythmic framework for the vocal performance. One never hears a *bàtá* player sing while he is playing. This is such a well-established cultural fact that it is captured in the proverb *Alubàtá kìí dárin* (a *bàtá* player is not known to initiate singing). In its conversational use, this proverb is employed to caution against stretching oneself beyond one's capability, not to take on too much, not to do too many things at the same time or not to try to be a 'jack of all trades'. Oyèlámì said that a *bàtá* player cannot drum and sing simultaneously as 'that would be double talking' (personal communication, 3 September 1999, Ìrágbìjí). In other words, an *alubàtá* cannot utter words while being in the cerebral process of encoding language onto the drum.

There are specific *bàtá* repertoires in which the drums do in fact accompany songs, such as *apidán* (a theatrical kind of Egúngún masquerade that specializes in character sketches), and quasi-secular masking traditions such as *alárìnjó* (also called *agbégijó*), an acrobatic performance, both of which are entertainment genres of masqueraders (from the Òjè lineage).[13] In this accompanying role, the *bàtá* plays what Àyándòkun refers to as 'pure rhythm'.

There are generic secular dance rhythms commonly accessed as song accompaniment, the best-known being rhythms called *gbàmùn* and *ìjó oge*. (The backing track that Àyándòkun laid down for the proverbs [☉ 1] is *ìjó oge*.) According to Àyándòkun, as the knowledge of the *bàtá* diminishes, these and other secular dance rhythms – which are considerably easier to play than more traditional repertoires – are becoming increasingly popular amongst both listeners and drummers. As the *bàtá* appears more in secular settings in regional areas such as Òyó (although not in urban centres) at weddings, naming ceremonies, funerals, cultural festivals and parties, much of the repertoire draws from generic, textless dance rhythms. Within these secular repertoires, the drummers, where appropriate, may superimpose textual repertoires such as personal *oríkì* and *òwe*. There is also a repertoire of sexual and abusive texts that *bàtá* drummers play for fun and entertainment. This repertoire is known as *efẹ àlujó apaniléẹrín* (humorous or abusive drum texts in dance rhythms).[14]

---

[13]   Òjè is the inherited craft lineage of masqueraders. Òjè members often intermarry with Àyàn drummers.

[14]   Táíwò Abímbọlá collected some sexual texts from Òyó *alubàtá* Jimọh Àyántáyọ̀. Two examples are: *Kìí ṣẹ jó alátònà bóbìnrin kò bá ní irun nídìí, kìí ṣe jó alátònà* [It is not the fault of the go-between if the woman introduced to you does not have pubic hair], and *Ẹni tósadó lósóríire, Ẹnìtójalè lóbọmọjẹ* [He who fucks is fortunate, he who steals is cursed].

There is a religious *bàtá* repertoire called the *ìlù ṣíṣẹ̀*, which is played very early in the morning before devotees arrive for a ceremony. The *ìlù ṣíṣẹ̀* functions to invoke the *òrìṣà* before the house fills with people and the rituals begin. The drummers can play for many *òrìṣà* in any given performance, and indeed when I witnessed a performance of the *ìlù ṣíṣẹ̀*, it began at 4 a.m. and lasted for more than two hours without a break, which gives an idea of the size of the liturgy. The *ìlù ṣíṣẹ̀* is not a fixed liturgy but is a fluid recitation of *òrìṣà* rhythms and may include any of the *òrìṣà* rhythms presented in this volume (or not). To my knowledge, as well as being regionally heterogeneous, the *ìlù ṣíṣẹ̀* would usually be marginally different with each performance of the same drummers, depending on the inspiration of the *ìyáàlù* player and the ceremonial context. The *ìlù ṣíṣẹ̀* is laden with text.

The *bàtá* does not always render text within traditional repertoires. Yet another repertoire is *àbìdà* which Àyándòkun describes as sacred dance rhythms for *òrìṣà*. There are five *àbìdà* rhythms, one each for Ṣàngó, Òrìṣà Oko, Erinlẹ̀, Ọya and Ṣọ̀pọ̀nnọ́, and, unlike most sacred repertoires, they are textless. One of the stylistic features is complex interlocking patterns between the *ìyáàlù* and the *omele abo*. The *àbìdà* provide dance accompaniment for sacred *òrìṣà* dances. It is now a little-known genre and, due to its complexity, many younger drummers do not know the repertoire. Àyándòkun regards *àbìdà* as one of the most endangered repertoires.

It is text-based repertoires that are the focus of this volume. The two most common textual genres are *oríkì* (loosely translated as praise poetry) and *òwe* (proverbs), both of which I explain in more detail in Chapter 2. While these two corpuses are often generic and are performed by Àyàn drummers who specialize in particular kinds of drum ensembles, some repertoires are specific to, or are stylized for, the *bàtá*. *Oríkì* and *òwe* repertoires straddle sacred and secular domains, while there is a religious repertoire that Àyándòkun simply calls '*òrìṣà* rhythms' or '*ìlù òrìṣà*', which are built on simple drum texts. Both *oríkì* and *òwe* may be interpolated into *òrìṣà* rhythms, as I will exemplify in Chapter 2.

Research Collaborators

With funding provided by the AHRC Research Centre, I was able to invite my two Nigerian research collaborators to the UK. The first was *alubàtá* Rábíù Àyándòkun, who provided the primary data, and the second was linguist and information scientist 'Túndé Adégbọlá, who contributed to the data analysis. Although my research has been most concentrated and continuous with Àyándòkun over the past ten years, I have worked with more than twenty Yorùbá drummers around Yorùbáland in Ọ̀yọ́, Ṣàgámù, Ògbómọ̀ṣọ́, Ìrágbìjí, Òṣogbo and Lagos. My contact with some of these drummers has been relatively fleeting, constituting a single conversation or interview. With other drummers, I have forged ongoing research relationships and they are therefore worthy of mention as research participants who have contributed to the current study over a longer period of time.

My first contact with a Yorùbá *bàtá* drummer was with Múráínà Oyèlámì, who gave me my very first *bàtá* lesson in London in June 1998, while he was visiting to work on a local arts project. We met again a few days later and had more time to talk. He kindly gave me a copy of his book, *Yorùbá Bàtá Music* (1991), which is a landmark text in terms of the study of the *bàtá* drum language. Best known as a visual artist, Oyèlámì had been working in academic environments prior to his 1991 publication, beginning as a theatre student at Ọbáfẹ́mi Awólọ́wọ̀ University, Ilé-Ifẹ̀ (then University of Ifẹ̀), where he went on to teach traditional music between 1975 and 1987. He was also the Guest Professor in African Studies at the University of Bayreuth, Iwalewa-Haus, Germany in 1981–82 and he has since done numerous residencies at universities around the world. I have maintained a relationship with Oyèlámì, who is more an analyst and teacher than a *bàtá* stage performer (as is Àyándòkun). Indeed, some of the ideas that are presented in this volume derive from conversations with Oyèlámì.

When I first arrived in Nigeria and went to Ọ̀yọ́, I began taking lessons from *alubàtá* Àyángbémiga Àyánwálé. Some of the proverbs that appear in this volume were first encountered in my 1999 lessons with Àyánwálé, although Àyándòkun performs them on the CD and I have presented transcriptions of Àyándòkun's versions. I have also maintained a working relationship with Àyánwálé. On that first trip to Ọ̀yọ́, I also met Jimọh Àyántáyọ̀, who, with the field assistance of Táíwò Abímbọ́lá, made recordings and text translations of the *omele mẹ́ta* in August 2007.

As all of the *alubàtá* I had worked with up until 2002 were Muslims (as are the vast majority of *alubàtá*), I was keen to locate traditionalist *alubàtá,* who are now rare. During a short research trip in April 2002, I heard about Àlàbí Ọ̀ṣúníyì Àdìgún Àyángbẹ́kún, a *bàtá* drummer who was a traditional *òrìṣà* priest and master diviner in Ògbómọ̀ṣọ́. I made the dangerous road trip from Ọ̀ṣogbo to Ògbómọ̀ṣọ́ where I was met with enthusiasm and generosity and was astounded by Àyángbẹ́kún's esoteric and textual knowledge and his recitation virtuosity. As a *bàtá* drummer whose family had never converted to Islam, Àyángbẹ́kún was a rare person with extraordinary religious knowledge. Hence, I did not study or even discuss the *bàtá's* music with Àyángbẹ́kún but on that and subsequent visits, I collected oral literature and esoteric information, some of which appears in this volume. I had planned to continue my research with Àyángbẹ́kún both for the current project and beyond, but tragically he died unexpectedly in early 2007. Less than fifty years old at the time of his passing, Àyángbẹ́kún's premature death was a terrible loss for those who knew him and to the wider *bàtá* research project. I am yet to hear of another *alubàtá* with his extraordinary breadth of spiritual knowledge.

Also worthy of mention is my ongoing research collaborator and friend Táíwò Abímbọ́lá. Our first encounter was in Havana, Cuba in March 1998, at which time I hired him as my Spanish-English translator while undertaking MMus research about the vestiges of drum language in the parallel Cuban *batá* drumming tradition. Abímbọ́lá invited me to his family home in Ọ̀yọ́ in July 1999 shortly after Nigeria became a democracy, and we have been firm friends and worked together ever since. As a divining priest with a keen interest in religious texts, Abímbọ́lá has been helping me with my research work by collecting religious texts and translating data. As an inherited priest in the alleged place of origin of the *bàtá* drum, he shares my passion about the *bàtá's* musical and textual tradition and has made a significant contribution to the current volume.

Over the past decade, I have spent many more hours working with Àyándòkun than any other single informant. I chose to bring him to the UK as my first research collaborator given this established working relationship, his encyclopaedic knowledge of the drum rhythms and texts, his high level of performance skill (which includes working in the recording studio) and the fact that he is fluent in English, which is rare among *alubàtá*. Àyándòkun and I have been working together since our stretch of fieldwork in September 1999. We have worked in Nigeria during my five visits there (26 July–9 September 1999, 25 July–13 September 2000, 6 August–14 September 2001, 2–12 April 2002 and 1 August–9 September 2003). We have also worked together in the UK and via telephone calls and emails. Àyándòkun began the work as my research collaborator in March–April 2007, at which time he came and stayed with me and worked at SOAS. This four-week period was spent taking lessons, conducting formal interviews and less formal conversations, collecting *ẹnà* data, checking and corroborating previous data I had collected from him and making studio recordings.

In discussions in London in March–April 2007, Àyándòkun felt that it was very important that I present his family history in order to put his *bàtá* playing and style into context. The following account is compiled from conversations with Àyándòkun and by cross-referencing his oral history with secondary sources (Lander 1965, Clapperton 1966, Johnson 1976, Smith 1988 and Klein 2000).

Àyándòkun's hometown, Èrìn-Ọ̀ṣun, was initially a refugee settlement. His family were originally located in Èrìnlé, a town close to Ìlọrin in current Kwara State. The mythological origin story of Èrìnlé is that it was founded by Ọbàlùfọn (the *òrìṣà* of cloth and weaving), who trekked north from the legendary birthplace of the Yorùbá progenitor, Odùduwà, in the city of Ilé-Ifẹ̀. At the time Àyándòkun's family lived in Èrìnlé, Ìlọrin was led by an Ọ̀yọ́ *kakanfo* (a term akin to 'field marshal') called Àfọ̀njá, whose grandfather, the *Baṣòrun* (prime minister) Gaha had founded Ìlọrin. Àfọ̀njá declared his independence from the central rule in Ọ̀yọ́, which indeed may have heralded the fall of the Ọ̀yọ́ empire, and in order to strengthen his hand, he invited a Muslim Fulani priest called Álímì (also known as Salih) to Ìlọrin from the northern town of Sókótó. Álímì brought his army of Hausa slaves (known as the *jama*) with him, which Àfọ̀njá fatefully recruited into his own army in Ìlọrin. The *jama* rose against Àfọ̀njá, Álímì took control of Ìlọrin and his sons went on to be leaders in the southward drive of the *jihad*.

According to Àyándòkun's narrative, when the war broke out between Àfọ̀njá and Álímì in Ìlọrin, the people of Èrìnlé supported Àfọ̀njá, who was 'an *òrìṣà* man' and

Illustration 1.3.   Chief Alhaji Rábíù Àyándòkun

'we were all Yorùbá people together'.[15] The Fulani invaded the towns surrounding Ìlọrin and raided Ẹ̀rìnlé in the middle of the night. According to Àyándòkun, his forefather was a warrior and palace *bàtá* drummer and heard the Fulani coming. He woke up everyone in the town (presumably with his *bàtá* drum) and warned the king, who was called Ọyágbọ́dùn. Àyándòkun's family still have this drum, which they refer to as *ìyáàlù ńlá* (big mother drum) although it is never taken out to play. Àyándòkun's family fled with the king and came to Ẹ̀rìn-Ọ̀ṣun to take refuge.[16] When the war in Ìlọrin was over, Ọyágbọ́dùn returned to Ìlọrin but left one of his sons in Ẹ̀rìn-Ọ̀ṣun to continue the kingship lineage. The current king of Ẹ̀rìn-Ọ̀ṣun (the *Ẹ̀lẹ́rìn* Ọba Yusuf Ọmọloyè Ọyágbọ́dùn II) is a descendant of Ọyágbọ́dùn, and to this day, despite the fact that he is a Muslim and there are less than a dozen *òrìṣà* devotees left in the town, he must hold a festival to honour Ọbàlùfọ̀n every June or July, at which time they ritually slaughter a cow. Àyándòkun's family are also still duty-bound to play for and protect the *Ẹ̀lẹ́rìn*. Àyándòkun is a close friend of the current king, who granted him a chieftancy title on 19 June 2004 called *Agbáṣà* Ẹ̀rìn-Ọ̀ṣun (the ambassador of culture in Ẹ̀rìn-Ọ̀ṣun).

As well as being a master *bàtá* drummer, Àyándòkun's father, Yusuf Ìgè Àyánsínà Àyándòkun, was a successful farmer and trader, which brought him considerable wealth. Àyándòkun's mother, Munirat Yusuf Àyándòkun (who is still alive and in her nineties) traded kola nuts with the Hausas and made and traded soap. Both of Àyándòkun's parents were *òrìṣà* devotees (his father Òrìṣà Òkò, the *òrìṣà* of farming, and his mother Ọ̀ṣun, the *òrìṣà* of fertility and the river) and they converted to Islam before Àyándòkun was born in 1958. When Àyándòkun was a few days old, they gave him a traditional Àyàn initiation first, and later called in the *imam* for his Muslim naming ceremony. Àyándòkun has been a practising Muslim for his whole life, although he upholds some of the traditional Àyàn rituals. He made the *hajj* to Mecca in 2001 but has nevertheless followed the same plural religious procedure with his own children, who all have both Àyàn and Muslim names.

All of Àyándòkun's forefathers were *bàtá* drummers and his father instigated Àyándòkun's long and involved training when he was just six years old. This

---

[15]   Àyándòkun's timeframe for the war in Ìlọrin and his family's exodus to Ẹ̀rìn-Ọ̀ṣun is four hundred years ago, which is at odds with written historical sources, which place the beginning of the *jihad* in 1798 and Àfọ̀njá's rule in Ìlọrin around 1830 (see Clapperton 1966:91). Despite the fact that the word Yorùbá was not applied as a collective term for the peoples now known as Yorùbá until the late nineteenth century, it is now common for contemporary Yorùbá people to cast the term back into time immemorial. As Vansina (1985:127–29) points out, concepts of time are culture-specific and may not conform to linear notions of time.

[16]   Klein (2000:36), whose account is at odds with Àyándòkun's, reports, 'Erin-Osun is said to have been founded by Prince Mosa Paayan from Ifẹ̀, who lead the people from Erin-Ile ... to what would become their sister-town of Erin-Osun' but does not state her source.

apprenticeship involved enormous personal sacrifice for the young Àyándòkun during a period of significant social and religious change in Nigeria in the post-independence period. In 1955, three years before Àyándòkun was born, free school education was introduced into southwest Nigeria, but drumming was not on the curriculum. In many regions, there were free school lunches for children, which provided an added incentive for people in lower economic brackets to send their children to school. Nevertheless, Àyándòkun, who was born into a drumming lineage, was taken out of school as a boy to work with his father as a ritual drummer. By the time Àyándòkun was an adolescent, playing in *òrìṣà* ceremonies was not fashionable in his social setting and, at times, performing publicly was humiliating for him. While his peers aspired to modernization, which included colonial schooling, escalating religious conversion to Islam and Christianity and the oppression of Yorùbá traditions, Àyándòkun was following what many saw as a backward path. To illustrate his difficulties, Àyándòkun shared a painful memory of playing for the *òrìṣà* Ṣọ̀pọ̀nnọ́ in the central market at Òṣogbo where he was approached by his peers saying, 'Why do you want to play for *òrìṣà*?'. In the midst of this adolescent turmoil, Àyándòkun's father called the thirteen-year-old Rábíù to his bedside on the day that he passed away and passionately asked his son to carry on and protect the *bàtá* tradition. Recognizing that the *bàtá* is an endangered tradition with a receding knowledge base, Àyándòkun has since been on a personal, and now international, mission to promote and preserve his heritage. Although his drumming skill and knowledge were hard-earned, his international success, status and prosperity are perhaps beyond even the most ambitious aspirations his father had for him.

Àyándòkun's father was a great friend of the German researcher and writer Ulli Beier, who has periodically resided in Òṣogbo since the late 1950s. Beier and his wife at the time, artist Susanne Wenger, became deeply involved with traditionalist priests, artists, writers and musicians. Together, Beier, Wenger and artist Georgina Beier (who had married Ulli in the 1960s) organized a cohort of local artists who collectively provided a powerful counterpoint to the oppressive forces against Yorùbá traditions described above. Beier first invited Àyándòkun and his senior brother Làmídì Àyánkúnlé to Germany in 1987 to perform in the National Museum in Berlin. Àyándòkun returned to Germany in 1989, without his brother, to run workshops for international young composers at the University of Bayreuth. As a result of the connections Àyándòkun made through Beier and through his travels, he has become amongst the most well-known Yorùbá *bàtá* drummers in the world. Beier reports (personal communication, Sydney, 12 April 2003) that Àyándòkun was the first Yorùbá master drummer he had encountered who had mastered both the *bàtá* and the *dùndún*, which are normally separate performance and drum-making specializations and are, even now, segmented into different family compounds. But it is the *bàtá* for which Àyándòkun is best known.

As well as touring (both in Nigeria and abroad) with his traditional group of drummers and masqueraders called simply *Yorùbá Bàtá*, Àyándòkun has also been deeply involved in popular music, initially with Nigerian artists including

King Sunny Adé, Hauja Bello, Prince Adékúnlé, Adé Afọláyan (also known as Adé Love), and Álímì and his Àpàlà Group. From the late 1980s, Àyándòkun started collaborating with foreign popular artists on a range of fusion projects, including the German group Embryo, the American jazz drummer Billy Cobham and the Norwegian jazz artist Terje Isungset. In the 1990s, with Ulli Beier's input (Klein 2007:75–6), Àyándòkun formed the fusion outfit *Okuta Percussion* with Ulli Beier's son, Túnjí. With their diverse musical expertise, the ensemble fused Yorùbá, Indonesian, Indian and Australian Aboriginal traditions. *Okuta Percussion* recorded three CDs, including a collaboration with Nobel Literature Prize winner Wọlé Ṣoyínká, and did concert tours of Europe and Asia.

Above and beyond these ventures in 'world music', Àyándòkun asserts himself as an authoritative cultural bearer of Yorùbá *bàtá* drumming. As the need for him and his family to play in *òrìṣà* rituals diminishes with the contracting *òrìṣà* community in Ẹ̀rìn-Òṣun specifically, and Nigeria generally, Àyándòkun has stated on numerous occasions that it is his activities outside of Nigeria that help him to preserve the tradition. On one occasion, he explicitly said,

> When we travel out, we play really traditional. We don't really play traditional here. That is the problem we have. If I want to travel to Germany now, I have to prepare for traditional [rhythms]. We play totally traditional there. ... But in our own land here, we don't play traditional much ... The people [here] don't listen. They say "What is this?" The people say, *"we don't understand a word you're saying"*. (italics mine) (personal communication, Ẹ̀rìn-Òṣun, 16 August 2001.)

Having moved away from the *bàtá's* traditional religious sphere, many Yorùbá listeners no longer have the contextual knowledge and familiarity with the *bàtá* needed to extract its idiomatic texts.

Àyándòkun's involvement with me since 1999, and in the 2007 project specifically, has been largely driven by his personal agenda for preservation and education. He is most interested in the recordings generated by this project, which he wants to pass on to his children and other young family members who have neither been able to undergo a long apprenticeship with a master drummer nor witness and participate in the regular *òrìṣà* ceremonies that constituted his own musical education.

As Àyándòkun is the primary music informant for this project, I present a study of his drumming style and his method of encoding Yorùbá speech. I do not set out to explain *bàtá* drum language generally, which may have regional variants and undoubtedly has stylistic features that vary from drummer to drummer. Although I do not attempt to make comparisons between Àyándòkun's style and that of other drummers and areas, it nevertheless needs to be stated that his style derives from Ọ̀yọ́ style *bàtá*. Although Euba (1990:217–18) claims that all drummers fundamentally mimic the spoken Ọ̀yọ́ dialect, Àyándòkun maintains that drummers play 'in different accents', although he has never given me examples of these subtle discrepancies, which are possibly only perceivable to native drummers. Àyándòkun has also said that proverbs may be rendered slightly differently across various regions. A more obvious difference between Ọ̀yọ́ style and Èrìn-Ọ̀sun style is that most (certainly the elder) Ọ̀yọ́ *alubàtá* play the large skin (*ojú òjò*) with the left hand, whereas Èrìn-Ọ̀sun drummers use the right hand, as in Ìséyìn. Despite the fact that Ọ̀yọ́, the alleged home of Ṣàngó and centre of *bàtá* drumming, is of enormous political import, Àyándòkun and his family in Èrìn-Ọ̀sun have managed to make their mark as the major cultural bearers of the contemporary *bàtá* tradition.

My second research collaborator, 'Túndé Adégbọlá, has injected the linguistic expertise essential to this project. Adégbọlá is the son of an eminent religious scholar and one-time bishop of the Methodist Church in Nigeria, the late E.A. Adé Adégbọlá. Unlike many Yorùbá Christians, and like his father, Adégbọlá junior has taken a keen and open-minded interest in Yorùbá traditions and the link between traditional technologies (such as medicine, music and divination) and science. His skill set and research interests are entirely different from, but complimentary to, those of Àyándòkun. Adégbọlá is an engineer and computer scientist with a PhD in Information Science from the University of Ìbàdàn, where he works as an Associate Lecturer at the Africa Regional Centre for Information Science. His research interests are focused on the use of information coding theory to investigate language. Working at the intersection of linguistics, music, probability theory and cognitive psychology, he has been researching the science behind the phenomenon of speech surrogacy and the use of talking drums among the Yorùbá.

Among his many projects, Adégbọlá is designing Automatic Speech Recognition (ASR) and Test To Speech (TTS) synthesis systems for African tone languages. He is Executive Director of African Languages Technology Initiative (Alt-i), which is a research and development organization with the aim of appropriating various aspects of Human Language Technologies (HLTs) for use in African languages. Partly funded by the Open Society Initiative for West Africa (OSIWA), the organization is at present involved in the development of computer keyboards, speech recognition, speech synthesis, optical character recognition and other HLT-based systems for various African languages.

Beyond the above research projects, Adégbọlá is best known in Nigeria for his film productions with one of the nation's most successful production houses, Mainframe. As a partner of Mainframe, Adégbọlá has produced and acted in many documentaries and cultural dramas, for which the company is most renowned. As a freelancer, Adégbọlá is currently initiating internationally funded community education projects and community radio networks in Senegal and Sierra Leone.

Adégbọlá plays music for pleasure, including the *dùndún*, acoustic guitar and keyboards. Occasionally he plays professionally and has produced several film soundtracks for Mainframe Films. Our collaboration on this research project pulls together Adégbọlá's passion for music, his interest in Yorùbá language and religious traditions and his scientific expertise. I brought Adégbọlá into the project to undertake Yorùbá-English translation, to contribute to the data analysis and to

Illustration 1.4.   'Túndé Adégbọlá

advise me on some of the technical linguistic analysis. His input has been most significant in the analysis of the ẹnà data. Together, we devised a theory for how ẹnà functions as an interface between the Yorùbá speaker and the *bàtá* drum. As a Yorùbá-speaking linguist and scientist, Adégbọlá has also offered insights about the musical data from an entirely different perspective to my analysis, as a foreign musician and ethnomusicologist. As someone outside of ethnomusicology, Adégbọlá's questions have also helped to make this volume accessible to scholars from other disciplines.

Chapter 2
An Extension of Mouth: How the *Bàtá* Talks

In my family, when I was born, I know my family plays the drums very well,
very neat. We do everything proper … In my family we want to use the drum to
talk clear to greet the *òrìṣà* and to greet the King, and the people as well .. Maybe
I can find some very old people at Ọ̀yọ́ who can do this thing, but most people
now at Ọ̀yọ́ just know how to play the type of the dance drum, some new thing.
This is the same in Ìbàdàn. In Ẹ̀rìn-Ọ̀ṣun, we do both. We don't want to forget.
Now if I don't work this out it is going to be lost. Not many people know now.
(Àyándòkun, London, 31 March 2007)

Àyándòkun made the above statement after viewing several hours of my audio-
visual field recordings from Ọ̀yọ́ (the alleged place of origin and cultural centre of
bàtá drumming), Ìrágbìjí and Òṣogbo. When assessing other drummers, Àyándòkun
is never ungenerous but is always dispassionate, giving credit where it is due and
offering an honest critique. In response to my fieldwork materials, he said he saw
only one old man who spoke well with the *bàtá,* as the younger *alubàtá* played only
textless dance rhythms. He reiterated his fear that the craft of talking with the *bàtá* is
not being passed on successfully and could easily be lost forever. This chapter is the
fruition of a ten-year collaboration driven by my long-held curiosity about how the
bàtá talks and Àyándòkun's desire that the system be known, taught and preserved.

Although Àyándòkun says he can talk clearly on the *bàtá*, he cannot always
clearly articulate how he encodes speech on the drum. When I interviewed Múráínà
Oyèlámì in September 1999 in his home in Ìrágbìjí, he agreed with me that *alubàtá*
are often not aware of the techniques they are applying when they speak with the
drum and therefore have trouble theorizing their craft. He said, 'It's part of him.
It's like an extension of mouth'. Like the complex, unconscious reflexes of speech,
a *bàtá* player does not go through a cognizant process in order to produce words
on the drum.

When I used to ask *alubàtá* questions about the drum language at the outset
of my research, they often looked at me blankly, not understanding my questions,
or else they spoke about how the drum talks in very general or metaphoric terms
such as 'the *ìyáàlù* talks and the *omele abo* follows'. I learned very quickly that
asking direct questions about what drummers do when they encode speech was
not reaping the kind of data I wanted. It became evident that *alubàtá* have little
conscious understanding of the grammar of their musical system and certainly
cannot articulate very much about it when questioned. Even Àyándòkun – who has
experienced years of interrogation from foreign drumming students and scholars

and is a master when speaking on the drum – often explains things in a way that appears to be in conflict with the research of Oyèlámì and myself. Of course, neither Oyèlámì nor Àyándòkun are wrong, but I have come to realize that when he plays, Àyándòkun's hands function like a speech organ, as Oyèlámì aptly put it, 'an extension of mouth'. Indeed, linguist Victor Manfredi, who has also been doing research on the *bàtá* drum language,[1] noticed that the larynxes of *alubàtá* move as they drum, yet they do not make any utterances while the drum is talking (personal communication, telephone, February 2004). Yorùbá boys destined for drumming begin to learn the syllables and hand movements at a very early age. While I am not making a cognitive study of the internal learning and playing processes of *alubàtá*, it appears that their hands are directly connected to the speech centre of the brain.

When we were making the recordings for this volume, I sat beside Àyándòkun and videoed his right hand from a range of angles. When I made a comment to him about the shapes and movements of his hand, he laughed and said, 'Don't ask me what I do. I don't know what I do.' This chapter endeavours to elucidate what Àyándòkun cannot explain about his own playing and to propose a rudimentary grammar of how he speaks with his *bàtá*. While I too still cannot explain everything that Àyándòkun does on the drum when he encodes speech, I cannot hope to offer a comprehensive grammar of his *bàtá* drumming style or *bàtá* drumming generally. What I can do in this chapter is add a considerable amount of new data to Oyèlámì's findings and present a more refined and detailed framework for what is at work when *alubàtá* use the drum as a speech surrogacy instrument. It is my hope that my findings will assist further research about *bàtá* drumming specifically, and speech surrogacy in drumming generally.

The *Bàtá's* Textual Repertoire

As set out in the first chapter, this volume concentrates on *oríkì* (praise poetry), *òwe* (proverbs) and *ìlù òrìṣà* (*òrìṣà* rhythms). For those readers who are unfamiliar with the *bàtá* and/or Yorùbá language, I recommend looking at the sections on notation choices and orthography in the preface before proceeding to read this chapter.

Oríkì (Praise Poetry)

Although *oríkì* is most commonly translated into English as 'praise poetry', these English words are a little misleading as *oríkì* are not always flattering. As the primary function of an *oríkì* is to detail the identity of its object, distinctive features and deeds – including negative ones – can emerge in an *oríkì* performance. Barber

---

[1]   Manfredi conducted research with Àyándòkun's brother, Làmídì Àyánkúnlé, but had not published his findings at the time of writing this volume.

(1990:315) describes *oríkì* as 'attributions or appellations: epithets, elaborated or concise, which are addressed to a subject and which are equivalent to, or alternatives to, names'. Drummers need to be versed in the many different kinds of *oríkì*. Textual knowledge, good social and ritual timing, taste and a highly developed sense of aesthetics are the primary distinguishing skills of a Yorùbá master drummer.

There are different categories of *oríkì*. They can be directed at the *òrìṣà*, the *Eégún* (ancestors), living humans, animals, town lineages (*oríkì orílè*), and even food and other inanimate objects. At both religious and secular events, a *bàtá* master may play the personal *oríkì* and/or *orílè* (the two genres are often interwoven) of individuals entering the ritual or social space. He may also target 'big men' and 'big women' (*ènìyàn ńlá*),[2] pouring copious praises on them and maybe even deprecating their rivals. As social ascendancy often intersects with material wealth, big men and women are obliged to exchange the drummers' praises for hard cash. Hence knowledge of individuals and their *oríkì* is essential to the livelihood of a drummer. As Wenger puts it:

> [T]he drummer must compensatively play the part of the 'sacred fool'. Even while carrying out a ritual obligation, his talking can include funny addresses to everyone in earshot with their proper *oríkì* and with allusions to their private matters. In order to be informed of these things, he is by profession also a gossip, carousing about the town at all hours (1983:203).

Oríkì can be played on all kinds of Yorùbá drums, but their rendering has reached the highest forms on the *dùndún* and the *bàtá*. All kinds of *oríkì* can be superimposed over sacred or secular rhythms, but perhaps their most potent rendering is through the solo performance in what Euba calls 'direct speech form',[3] which I call 'direct speech mode'. Within the *bàtá* repertoire, direct speech mode is only rendered on the solo *ìyáàlù* (see Example AII.2–11, ⊙ 2–21 for *oríkì òrìṣà*).

---

[2] See Barber (1981) for the social and economic dynamics of Yorùbá big men and women.

[3] Euba's classification of the speech modes of the *dùndún* are applicable and useful to the study of *bàtá* surrogate speech. To summarise the three forms he proposes: i) *Direct speech form* – heightened speech in free rhythm; ii) *Musical speech form* – heightened speech in strict rhythm. This surrogate speech form must conform to an underlying regular pulse, and 'there is a combined speech-musical function, in which the text is neither entirely speech-realized nor entirely music-realized'; and iii) *Song form* – the drum 'may be used to imitate a voice singing a literary text'. In this form, the drum's 'speech function may be considered as having been assimilated into its musical function'. In other words, the drum copies the pitches and rhythm of a melody. This is more applicable to the variable-pitch and sustaining *dùndún*, which can more adequately imitate a singing voice than the staccato *bàtá* can.

Every *oríkì* performance is slightly different, as is the oral performance of *oríkì*. The master drummer constructs each rendering by making split-second decisions about which phrase will follow another. For example, there is a substantial repertoire of segments of text that describe and praise the *òrìṣà* Àyàn. The drummer will draw from his internalized repertoire of text segments according to his inspiration in the moment. There will be certain phrases that almost always appear, while others may frequently or occasionally appear, or may emerge in different moments in the linear organization. Nevertheless, there is a rough form for each *oríkì*. While phrases can be switched or left out entirely, some phrases commonly appear at particular approximate points of an *oríkì* performance. Àyándòkun will usually open with the same phrase, and the closing is almost always around the words *ṣe pẹ̀lẹ́* (sometimes with repeated renderings of *pẹ̀lẹ́*), which can be variously translated as 'go gently', 'take it easy' or 'peace'. *Ṣe pẹ̀lẹ́* can also appear anywhere in the rendition, but its final statement is played slightly slower and in a declamatory fashion. As well as closing the *oríkì*, the words *ṣe pẹ̀lẹ́* give a signal to the other *bàtá* drummers that they are about to enter with the *ìlù òrìṣà*.

Whenever an Àyàn drummer picks up the drum to play (be he an *alubàtá* or *aludùndún*), he will play the individualized *oríkì* of his father and other Àyàn ancestors, closely followed by *oríkì* Àyàn. Àyándòkun follows this practice whether he is starting an *òrìṣà* ceremony, playing on a concert stage, sitting down to a lesson, starting the day in the recording studio or even picking up the drum on his own at home. The Àyàn drummer must pay homage to the drummers who came before him, no matter what the context of his drumming.

As well as being rendered in direct speech mode, the same *oríkì* phrases can also be organized into rhythms and can be played over *òrìṣà* rhythms, such as in *ìlù* Ògún (see Example 2.2, ☉ 22). In this scenario, the *oríkì* is not performed in length, but the *ìyáàlù* player extracts certain segments of it. The *omele abo* player can join in if he knows the *oríkì* text (which he can never do in direct speech mode). The *ìyáàlù* can also 'converse' with vocal *oríkì* performers by interpolating words and phrases (in direct speech mode) in response to, and in between, their utterances.[4]

Òwe (Proverbs)

Another important text-based repertoire accessed by Yorùbá drummers is *òwe*. *Òwe* are not drummed in direct speech mode but are rendered over danceable rhythms – that is, musical speech mode.

Yorùbá speakers frequently use *òwe* in ordinary conversation. Partly for this reason, *òwe* are easily recognizable to modern Yorùbá speakers when rendered on

---

[4]　The *bàtá* can function in this conversational way across various other genres of oral literature such as Ṣàngó *pípè* (a liturgy particular to Ṣàngó devotees), *ìjálá* (the oral literature of hunters) and *ewì* (a form of Egúngún oral literature).

the drum, in comparison with the increasingly obscure *oríkì* and *òrìṣà* texts. As with *oríkì*, *òwe* can be superimposed over *òrìṣà* rhythms or secular dance rhythms, although they are not performed by the solo *ìyáàlù* in direct speech mode as *oríkì* frequently are. *Òwe*, whether played on the *bàtá* or another Yorùbá drum, can vary rhythmically, although they do tend to be set to generic rhythmic frameworks, and hence are partly recognizable through their rhythm.[5] Some *òwe* are idiomatic to *òrìṣà* rhythms, while others are more secular in nature. Drummers can choose to play *òwe* to reflect something happening in the social situation, such as the presence of two rival big men. The drummers may also direct their *òwe* at rivals of their own, most usually drummers. Using coded texts, drummers have the power to say what would be socially unacceptable to articulate.

Some *òwe* are idiomatic to the *dùndún* and are not generally played by the *bàtá*.[6] Others can be played on the *bàtá*, *dùndún* or other Yorùbá drums, but might be rendered slightly differently within each ensemble. Nevertheless, there is usually an internal, musical rhythmic patterning that derives from the spoken words. For example, compare AII.1 (☉ 1 and ☉ 32), which are different renditions of the same *òwe* on the *ìyáàlù bàtá* and the *omele méta* respectively.

Listening to these recordings, one of the interesting things that emerges is that when Àyándòkun precedes the drummed texts with vocal renditions, his voice imitates the sound of the drum. His *bàtá* vocal recitals are more like ordinary Yorùbá speech, whereas his *dùndún* recitals are slower and exaggerate the pitch contours and tone glides of speech. Hence we observe a two-way mimicking: speech mimics the drum, just as the drum mimics speech.

In a *bàtá* performance context, when the *ìyáàlù* begins to play an *òwe*, the *omele abo* player joins in when he can (see below for more details about how this actually manifests itself in performance). In different *bàtá* performances, the rhythmic structure can vary slightly or significantly. As Example 2.1 shows, the word structure, order, rhythm and/or content of the *òwe*, and even the strokes (see *mó* in bar 7), can change from one performance to another. Often, whole lines are rhythmically displaced (as in bars 12–15). Common variations are that the first line of the *òwe* may or may not be repeated, or the *ìyáàlù* can interject *bẹ́ẹ̀ ni* (yes)

---

[5]   European songs can also be recognised by their rhythm alone. I have conducted many experiments with my music students and have found the melodies (and hence their words) are more readily recognisable with a clapped rhythm than they are when the melody notes are sung or played in the correct succession but with a scrambled rhythmic structure. This must be largely due to the fact that the words of stress languages are co-ordinated to musical stresses. The same cannot be said of Yorùbá texts, which are primarily organised by relative pitch rather than stress.

[6]   'Túndé Adégbọlá gave me a booklet containing 230 drum texts (Ọládàpọ̀ 1995). While in London in March–April 2007, Àyándòkun studied this booklet and said that most of the texts are for *dùndún* and would not normally be played on the *bàtá*. However, he chose several *òwe* from the booklet that overlap with the *bàtá* repertoire for the April 2007 recordings.

Example 2.1.   Two different *ìyáàlù* performances of an *òwe* by Àyándòkun (*Òwe* 23, ☉ 1)

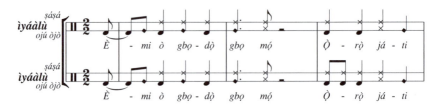

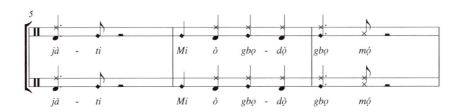

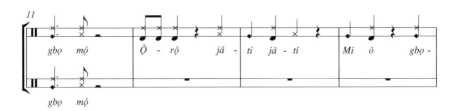

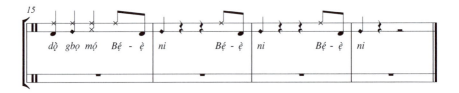

once, any number of times, or not at all. In Appendix II, the translations at the end of the *òwe* musical transcriptions are based on the *ìyáàlù* performance. As one can see from the transcription (Example AII.1), Àyándòkun often arranged the text in the *omele méta* performance differently from the *ìyáàlù* performance.

Ìlù Òrìṣà (Òrìṣà Rhythms)

There is an extensive and diverse repertoire of rhythms which are played in cult settings for the *òrìṣà* which are generally referred to as *ìlù òrìṣà*. I recorded and transcribed just sixteen *ìlù òrìṣà* for analysis while I could only include ten examples in the text and CD due to space constraints.

While ceremonies are normally in honour of one *òrìṣà*, such events are attended by *òrìṣà* devotees from different cults. Hence, in any one event, the drummers honour a range of devotees and their tutelary *òrìṣà*. These rhythms are played to communicate directly with the *òrìṣà*, who are said to recognize their own rhythms and to hear the texts being played. *Ìlù òrìṣà* also provide accompaniment for ritual dance, which can invoke spirit possession. When an *òrìṣà* possesses the body of a dancing devotee, it is believed that it is the *òrìṣà* dancing, not the devotee.

Each *ìlù òrìṣà* is preceded by the *oríkì*, played by the *ìyáàlù* in direct speech mode. When the *alubàtá* plays '*pèlé pèlé*' in a declamatory manner, this is a signal that the *ìlù òrìṣà* is about to begin and the other drummers join in. The *ìlù òrìṣà* Àyándòkun taught me were often considerably different from the versions he played in the recordings. While he would often teach me a skeleton rhythm that had strokes that coincided closely with a text, in his own performance he improvized around these skeletal rhythms, often adding or changing strokes and slightly obscuring the text. As with the *oríkì* transcriptions, the *ìlù òrìṣà* transcriptions I present below are made from the London recordings rather than from our lessons.

Most of the *ìlù òrìṣà* I have collected are constructed from simple, repeated drum texts, usually (although not always) containing the *òrìṣà's* name. These core texts tend to vary greatly in complexity. *Ìlù Ọbèdú* is comprised of a short text only containing the *òrìṣà's* name and his town of origin, Ọbà (Example 2.26), while some *ìlù òrìṣà* only contain the name of the *òrìṣà*, such as Ọbàlùfọn (Example 2.27), although Àyándòkun said that 'nobody' could remember the second segment of the Ọbàlùfọn text (in bars 2 and 4 of the transcription). He has taught me other *ìlù òrìṣà* where he has stated, 'It may be talking, but I'm not sure' or, 'nobody knows the text anymore'.

Performances of *ìlù òrìṣà* do not normally stick to the core text but may diverge into other texts such as *oríkì* and *òwe*, which can be superimposed over the basic rhythm, although two texts are not usually rendered simultaneously. For example, listen to Àyándòkun's recorded performance of Ògún (Example 2.2, ☉ 22). I have only done musical transcriptions for the first two *oríkì* and included the entire text after Example 2.2. I asked Àyándòkun to record a voice-over to help the listener follow the text. He often entered with the voice slightly late as he was

Example 2.2.   *Ìlù* Ògún (☉ 22)

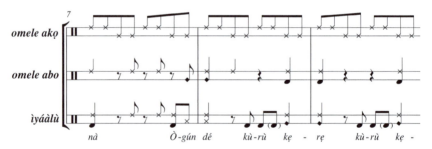

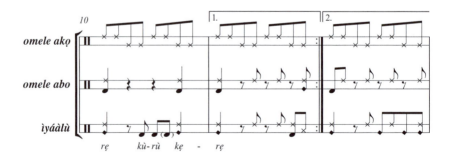

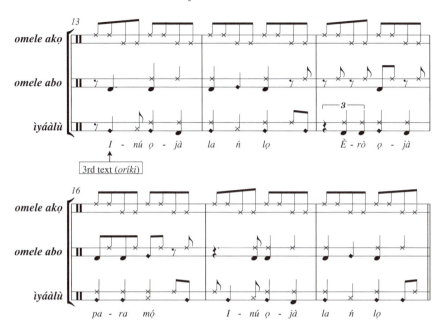

following the drums while he was overdubbing, so I have marked brackets around the unspoken text in the musical transcription. Àyándòkun starts with the basic rhythm (*şá di di*) and then interpolates *oríkì* segments between cycles of the basic rhythm. (The bracketed notes in bars 2, 4, 8, 9 and 10 of the transcription indicate variations in the repetition.) The texts in *ìlù* Ògún (☉ 22) are as follows:

First text (basic rhythm)
Şá di di şà di di

Second text (*oríkì*)
(Ògún feṛ́e) bí onílé
Ògún feṛ́e bí olóṇà
Ògún dé kùrù kẹré kùrù kẹré
Kùrù kẹré

Third text (*oríkì*)
Inú ọjà la ńlọ
Èrò ọjá para mọ́
(Inú ọjà la ńlọ)

Fourth text (*oríkì*)
Wòrú o Wòrú oko
Wòrú o Wòrú odò

Wòrú pakà féṛé jẹ
Mo délé morò fún baba
Babá na Wòrú jọjọ
Lábẹ́ ọ̀gẹ̀dẹ̀
Lábẹ́ òròńbò
O ti şe dábẹ́ ata
Idẹ wéṛé ni tÒşun
Òjé gùdùgbà ni tÒrìşà
Şéḳéşeḳè ni tÒgún
Ẹ bá mi kìlọ̀ fún baálẹ̀
Kó bá mi módòdó pakájà
Gbogbo wa lÒgún jọbí

(Return to *şá di di şà di di* x 4)

Fifth text (*oríkì*)
(Baba gbé şàdidi wá)

Mi ò rà ni mo wí
Baba gbé şàdidi wá
Mi ò rà ni mo wí
Baba gbé şàdidi wá

(Return to *şá di di şà di di* x 7)

(Change of rhythm to *àgèrè*)

Sixth text (*òwe*)
(Ibi ọká bá ba sí,) ìrẹ̀ ò gbọdọ̀
han

Interestingly, the same fragments of *oríkì* can be played for different *òrìṣà*. For example, the fourth text, which starts with '*Wòrú o Wòrú oko*', was also played in the *ìlù* Ọ̀ṣun, word for word (compare ⊙ 22 and ⊙ 23). (See App. II.12 for both drum texts with full translations).[7] Both examples for Ọ̀gún and Ọ̀ṣun illustrate what happens in a performance context, whereby texts are fluid and can be ordered variously within any given performance, and can also cross between different *òrìṣà* repertoires. As *ìlù* Ọ̀gún and *ìlù* Ọ̀ṣun illustrate, the *ìlù* *òrìṣà* repertoire is particularly interesting because different repertoires of texts can converge in this medium. Even the personal *oríkì* of an individual entering the ritual space can be superimposed over *ìlù òrìṣà*. Hence, *ìlù òrìṣà* are extremely variegated in their performance and no two renditions would be exactly the same, even within a specific regional tradition as performed by the same drummer. These two CD tracks also exemplify the complexity and virtuosity of extended text renditions. All of the other *ìlù òrìṣà* examples that follow were stripped down to their bare minimum; the transcribed examples only give the basic rhythmic framework at the beginning of each performance before Àyándòkun starts playing variations. We agreed that this was a helpful strategy to help the reader understand the construction of the rhythms.

This fluidity of rendering texts extends to every aspect of the *bàtá's* repertoire and is one of the primary reasons why it has been so difficult to make a concentrated study of *bàtá* speech surrogacy. Each of these three repertoires (*oríkì*, *òwe* and *ìlù òrìṣà*) has unique and distinctive features. It is the fact that the *ìyáàlù* renders speech in solo and in direct speech mode that it provides important data in this discussion. *Òwe* provide a particularly useful data source for a study of how ordinary speech is set to rhythmic music and particularly how the *omele abo* operates, while *ìlù òrìṣà* are most interesting for exploring how texts constitute the framework for actual rhythms.

A Critique of Previous Literature on the *Bàtá*'s Drum Language

As very little has been written about the *bàtá* drum language, several misconceptions have been circulated, recycled and left unchallenged. The source of some of this misinformation derives from Thieme (1969:173–214). In fairness to Thieme, he undertook a wide study of Yorùbá musical instruments with virtually no prior research or secondary resources. Nevertheless his thesis, and most particularly his chapter about the *bàtá*, are enormously valuable for any *bàtá* study. His description of how the drum talks is only one aspect of his *bàtá* chapter and he

---

[7] This particular text segment is particularly interesting as it seems to be a generic text that straddles different corpuses such as *oríkì* and divination texts from Ifá and the *dínlógún*. Segments of this text correspond to a song for Ochún in the Cuban *oricha* repertoire, which is accompanied by the *bàtá*: *ide were were ide Osun o, ide were were* x 2, *ide iyá, Ocha kinigua ide Osun, cheke cheke ide iyá, ide were were*.

evidently did not have the time to undertake a deep study or corroborate what his informants told him. I have analysed Thieme's transcriptions carefully and have had the opportunity to cross-reference the material with Àyándòkun, Adégbọlá and linguist Akínwùnmí Ìṣọlá. Space does not allow me to detail the problems with the transcriptions and analysis here, but below is a summary of Thieme's apparent misconceptions.

Thieme has not only named the drums of the *bàtá* ensemble incorrectly, ascribing one of the talking drums as 'omele abo iya'lu' and a non-semantic accompanying drum as 'omele abo', but there are also frequent errors and ambiguities in his (or his informants') Yorùbá orthography and tone markings, which have prevented an accurate analysis. Furthermore, Thieme has misunderstood non-semantic drum vocables as being part of a drummed proverb text and has included the non-semantic material in his analysis of the semantic text. Added to this, he seemed unaware of the various strokes on the *ojú òjò* of the *ìyáàlù* and *omele abo,* and has ascribed only one kind of stroke to both *ojú òjò* in his transcription. In mapping the problematic orthography onto the redacted strokes, Thieme has incorrectly ascribed the drum strokes to particular speech tones.

Thieme's notions that the *omele abo* 'follows' the *ìyáàlù,* and that texts are somehow segmented between the *ìyáàlù* and *omele abo,* have been an enduring misconception, reiterated uncritically by Bankole *et al.* (1975:55) and Klein (2000:42). Thieme states, 'An important use of the <u>iya'lu bata</u> and the <u>omele abo iya'lu</u> is as a pair of 'talking' instruments. … a particular phrase may be broken up into two or more elements which are then shared by the two drums. The two play complementary parts: the <u>iya'lu</u> leads, and the <u>omele abo iya'lu</u> responds' (174). Although Thieme's description of the roles of the *ìyáàlù* and *omele abo* is inaccurate and even misleading, his call/response description of the *ìyáàlù* and *omele abo* resembles the way the two lead drums of the Cuban *batá* ensemble (*iyá* and *itótele*) function. As the breaking up of text between the *ìyáàlù* and *omele abo* is not actually exemplified in Thieme's transcription and analysis, one wonders if he was influenced by literature about the Cuban *batá,* such as that of Ortiz (1955) and Rouget (1965), both of whom he quotes in other parts of his chapter (193). This particular misconception that the *omele abo* follows the *ìyáàlù* may also derive from an English mistranslation. As I will explain in more detail below, the *omele abo* player does 'follow' the *ìyáàlù* in the sense that he joins in after recognizing the text played on the *ìyáàlù.* Therefore, it follows temporally but not canonically or antiphonally. Strictly speaking, the *omele abo* accompanies the *ìyáàlù* by playing the same segments of text at the same time. The misunderstanding that it 'follows' may derive from the way Yorùbá-speakers use the English word 'follow'. While native English speakers understand 'follow' to mean 'come or go after' (in order of time), Yorùbá speakers frequently use the English word 'follow' to mean 'accompany'. Hence, when a Yorùbá speaker says, 'Let me follow you to Lagos', he probably means, 'let me come in the car with you' whereas a native English speaker may think he means travelling in the car behind. To apply this analogy to the *bàtá* ensemble, the *omele abo* accompanies the *ìyáàlù* like a passenger in the same car.

Let us turn our attention to Oyèlámì's analysis, along with my fine-tuning of his observations. Oyèlámì, who is clearly advantaged over foreign scholars as a native speaker of Yorùbá and as a cultural insider, collected much of his data from Àyándòkun and his senior brother Làmídì Àyánkúnlé (personal communication, Àyándòkun) and formulated some basic rules about how Yorùbá speech is mapped onto the *bàtá*. Oyèlámì also invented a TUBS notation[8] for the *bàtá*, in order to represent the various hand strokes employed on the *ojú òjò*. Using Oyèlámì's analysis, I have compiled a table that presents his preliminary data (see Table 2.1).

Table 2.1.   Oyèlámì's scheme for vowel encoding

Vowel type & speech tone	Drum	Drum stroke
'intense' vowel on a low (L) tone *à, è, ẹ̀, ò, ọ̀, àn, ẹ̀n, ọ̀n*	*ìyáàlù*	open tone with *ṣáṣá*
	omele abo	none
'soft' vowel on a low tone *ì, ù, ìn, ùn*	*ìyáàlù*	open tone
	omele abo	none
'intense' vowel on a mid (M) tone *a, e, ẹ, o, ọ, an, ẹn, ọn*	*ìyáàlù*	muted tone with *ṣáṣá*
	omele abo	open tone
'soft' vowel on a mid tone *i, u, in, un*	*ìyáàlù*	muted tone
	omele abo	open tone
'intense' vowel on a high (H) tone *á, é, ẹ́, ó, ọ́, án, ẹ́n, ọ́n*	*ìyáàlù*	slap mute with *ṣáṣá*
	omele abo	muted tone
'soft' vowel on a high tone *í, ú, ín, ún*	*ìyáàlù*	slap mute
	omele abo	muted tone
'improvized' tones *lá* or *já*	*ìyáàlù*	*ṣáṣá* (solo)
	omele abo	muted tone

In summary, Oyèlámì correctly tells us that the *ìyáàlù* can play the low, mid and high tones of the Yorùbá language (which is why it is the only *bàtá* drum in

---

[8]   Time Unit Box System notation was developed by Philip Harland at UCLA and is designed to notate percussion with a graphic representation of sounds in time and space. (See Koetting 1970.)

the traditional ensemble that can articulate in solo[9]), while the *omele abo* can play mid and high speech tones (which is why it is dependent on the *ìyáàlù*, as it cannot render low tones). Although the *ìyáàlù* can speak alone, the *omele abo* greatly enhances the overall intelligibility by further heightening the contrasts between the low tone (played with an *ìyáàlù* open stroke) and the mid tone (played with an *omele abo* open stroke). With its higher overall pitch, the *omele abo* is particularly suitable for marking the two higher tones.

Where Oyèlámì's work is perhaps the most innovative is in recognizing that the *bàtá* renders different kinds of vowels with different stroke combinations. In his text, Oyèlámì states, 'Vowels i̱ and u̱ are soft sound [*sic*] while the rest are open and more stressed' (1991:5). By 'the rest', he means *a, e, ẹ, o, ọ* and their nasalized equivalents. He also refers to these 'stressed' vowels as 'intense' vowels in the text and 'harsh' vowels in our conversations. In his text, he points out that the *ìyáàlù* marks intense vowels on any tone with a stroke on the *ṣáṣá* (thus using both skins), while the 'soft' vowels are only marked by strokes on the *ojú òjò*. Adding *ṣáṣá* strokes, which are sharper and louder than the *ojú òjò*, has the effect of creating musical stresses,[10] which may be why Oyèlámì also calls 'intense' vowels 'stressed' vowels. He also told me that he calls *i* and *u,* and their nasalized renderings, 'soft' vowels because 'what they have in common is the fact that the vowels *i* and *u* are similar when you think of softness … when you don't have the *bílálà* together with it' (personal communication, Ìrágbìjí, 3 September 1999). As Oyèlámì correctly points out, *i* and *u* are rendered on the *ìyáàlù* only on the lower, more mellow-sounding *ojú òjò,* without a simultaneous *ṣáṣá* stroke; therefore these soft vowels have a considerably lower transient and general amplitude than other vowel renderings that combine both skins. It appears that Oyèlámì calls *i* and *u* 'soft' vowels because of how they sound when played on the *ìyáàlù*, rather than drawing from observations about spoken Yorùbá or any linguistic terminology.

On looking at much earlier drafts of my research in the late 1990s, linguist and ethnomusicologist David Hughes[11] pointed out that Oyèlámì was accessing some universal acoustic linguistic principles. When I went to see Oyèlámì in September 1999 and shared some of Hughes' ideas with him, Oyèlámì said that he was not aware of the linguistics literature and theories and had arrived at his analysis and terminology without any secondary sources and in relative isolation, which makes his (Oyèlámì's) work all the more remarkable.

---

[9]   As I explain in the Chapter 3, the *omele mẹta* – a relatively new constellation within the *bàtá* ensemble – has three heads and can also speak on its own.

[10]   As well as the *bílálà* creating stresses in relation to the *ojú òjò* and the musical pulse, there is also an enormous dynamic range in how strokes are rendered on each skin, although I have not notated or analysed stress and any significance it may have in how speech is mimicked.

[11]   Hughes specializes in Japanese and Indonesian music. He has a particular interest in cross-cultural drum vocables, mnemonics and speech surrogacy. As my MMus and PhD supervisor, he has engaged with my research up to the current time.

Hughes (1989, 2000) presents an accurate description in phonetic terms of the relationship between vowel types, *solfège* and music mnemonics and found some remarkable cross-cultural parallels in how vocables and mnemonics function. He states, 'the principles behind acoustic-iconic systems (though not their precise application) are universally accessible to human experience' (2000:94). He points out that vowels have three characteristics, what phoneticians call their Intrinsic Pitch, Intrinsic Duration and Intrinsic Intensity. Hughes explains, 'each normal voiced vowel appears as a fundamental (the pitch at which the vocal chords vibrate) plus various relatively dense regions of overtones reflecting that vowel's characteristic resonance pattern (just as for a musical instrument). These latter regions are called formants, and they are crucial to "forming" the vowel's acoustic profile' (2000:98). Reiterating some of his published findings in his 1989 article, Hughes presents a diagram (reproduced in Illustration 2.1) which illustrates the approximate shape of the vocal tract for the vowel [i].

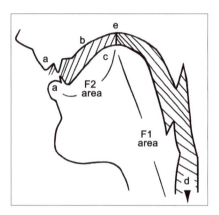

Illustration 2.1.   Shape of the vocal tract for vowel [i]

(a = lips; b = palate; c = tongue; d = to the larynx; e = point of maximum constriction)

Note: Illustration taken from *No Nonsense: The Logic and Power of Acoustic-iconic Mnemonic Systems* by David W. Hughes (Ethnomusicology Forum, 1 Jan 2000, Taylor & Francis). Reprinted by permission of the publishers (Taylor & Francis Group, http://www.informaworld.com).

Explaining the illustration, Hughes writes, 'The deeper chamber, marked 'F1 [first formant] area', can be called the throat cavity, and the other (F2 – second formant) the mouth cavity' (98). While the tension of the vocal chords forms the fundamental pitch of vowels (Intrinsic Pitch), their recognizable characteristics are formed in the first and second resonating chambers (Intrinsic Intensity). Hughes discovered that so-called 'nonsense syllables' are consistently ordered when used in cross-cultural *solfège* systems in the following order (from high to low) [i], [e], [a], [o], and [u]. The specific aspect of pitch *solfège* and vowel ordering is not relevant to Yorùbá singing and drumming, as Yorùbá vowels are distributed across the three relative tone levels. Thus *i* frequently falls on a spoken, sung or drummed low tone, while *u* frequently falls on a spoken, sung or drummed high tone. It is Hughes' findings about Intrinsic Intensity that are most relevant to my *bàtá* research. In line with Oyèlámì's own aural observations about the *bàtá*, Hughes goes on to point out:

> Phoneticians have found that in the vast majority of languages the vowels closest to [i] and [u], those spoken with the mouth relatively closed, will take less time to articulate and will also register a lower volume on a vU meter than will more open vowels; by contrast, the 'longest' and 'loudest' vowel is [a], followed by [o] and [e]. This is why [i] and [u] are often favoured for short notes or those in weak metric positions in oral mnemonic systems, while [a] tends toward the opposite.' (105–6).

What Oyèlámì is calling the 'softness' of the Yorùbá vowels *i* and *u* actually refers to a universal principle of their lower Intrinsic Intensity and their lower amplitude due to the shape of the vocal tract when they are uttered. While these vowels take less time for a human to utter, they also take less time for an *alubàtá* to play, as he only uses the strong hand to do so. Hughes also observes that the so-called 'close' vowels have a tendency to have shorter duration than more open vowels (such as [a]) and thus are said to have a shorter intrinsic duration. He summarizes, 'Perhaps because of these two features, there is a slight tendency for *i* and *u* in solfege to occur more often in metrically or dynamically weak positions, for example grace notes' (1989:13). As I will illustrate, the second part of a Yorùbá tone glide is placed in a metrically weak position when it is drummed and is represented by the vocable *i*.

I must make one more important point about the spoken Yorùbá language and the different uses of terminology by linguists and musicians, relating to how the language is mimicked by or encoded by a drum. Linguistic literature says that Yorùbá is a three-tone language. 'Tone' is a term that linguists use to describe pitch frequencies and is used interchangeably with the word 'pitch', whereas musicians use the word tone to describe timbre or the overtone content of a sound. However, when a linguist says that a true tone language has three tones, as in Yorùbá, he is not saying that only three pitches are used to speak the language. Rather, the linguist is referring to a model of three relative pitches. In an objective sense, as in all languages, Yorùbá speakers routinely *glissando* between the different pitches of syllables. Furthermore, the three relative pitches of Yorùbá constantly shift in ordinary speech. This means that the lowest and highest pitches of utterances, along with every frequency in between, are available to and used by a Yorùbá speaker. Therefore, the language is only conceptually made up of three tones or pitches, but they are not three tones or pitches in any objective sense. Although I cannot address this problem in detail or with any linguistic rigour in this volume, it becomes relevant when speaking of encoding speech onto a drum. As the next section explains, the *bàtá* conceptualizes these three relative speech pitches with different stroke combinations, but as the next chapter explains, the *dùndún* is not limited to three fixed pitch frequencies or sounds, and can therefore mimic the tonal shifts of ordinary Yorùbá speech.

Towards a Grammar of the *Bàtá's* Speech Surrogacy System

As I made my own transcriptions in conventional notation of Oyèlámì's TUBS transcriptions, I noticed several exceptions to his own scheme. As I collected an increasing body of *bàtá* drummed texts and *ẹnà*[12] data, I noticed many more anomalies than those appearing in Oyèlámì's transcriptions and I began to see emerging patterns. Here are some of my findings.

The *Ìyáàlù*

1. The *ìyáàlù* only consistently articulates all three tones in direct speech mode, such as when it is playing solo *oríkì*.

2. When the *ìyáàlù* is accompanied by the *omele abo* in musical speech mode, the *ìyáàlù* often does not articulate the mid tone on the *ojú òjò* (or at all), but leaves it to the *omele abo's* open tone. See Example 2.3, where the low and mid tones are divided between the *ìyáàlù* and *omele abo* large skins in bars 2 and 3. In bars 3 and 4 of the transcription, the *ìyáàlù* plays variations that articulate the mid tone, but the *omele abo* stays on the same pattern.

3. As exemplified by Example 2.4, the *ṣáṣá* is never played on syllables containing the soft vowels *i* and *u*, which have the lowest Intrinsic Intensity. Conversely, the *ṣáṣá* is usually played on syllables containing *a,* which have the highest Intrinsic Intensity, but may be dropped in the case of glides. However, the *ṣáṣá* is frequently eliminated on *o, ọ, e* and *ẹ,* which are in the middle of the Intrinsic Intensity spectrum. Returning to Hughes' observations, he notes, 'vowels closest to [i] and [u], those spoken with the mouth relatively closed, will take less time to articulate and will also register a lower volume on a vU meter than will more open vowels; by contrast, the 'longest' and 'loudest' vowel is [a], followed by [o] and [e]' (2000:105). Hence, the inclusion or exclusion of the *ṣáṣá* conforms with the acoustic properties of vocal production.

4. When playing in musical speech mode, the high tone is also often not explicitly rendered by either the *ìyáàlù* or *omele abo ojú òjò*. In Example 2.4, Àyándòkun often plays the slap tone on *jáde* as a touch tone, or leaves it out entirely while the *omele abo* also does not mark the high tone. One often hears a three-way division, with the low tone on the *ìyáàlù ojú òjò*, the mid tone on the

---

12   The *ẹnà* of *bàtá* players is a complex of vocables that stand in for Yorùbá syllables; it can instruct drummers how to play words on the drum and can also be used as a vernacular. (I expand on *ẹnà* in Chapter 4). Some of the examples in this section are garnered from *ẹnà* vocabulary rather than *bàtá* texts.

omele abo open tone and the high tone on the *ìyáàlù ṣáṣá*. In this example, we also see slightly staggered entries between the two talking drums on *Ẹ*.

Example 2.3.   *Ìlù* Ọya (☉ 24)

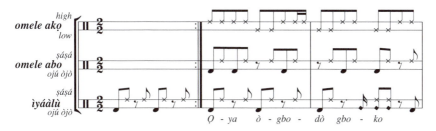

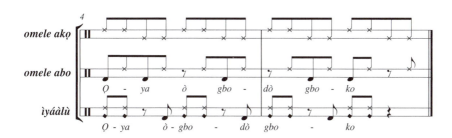

Example 2.4.   *Ìlù* Ṣàngó (☉ 25)

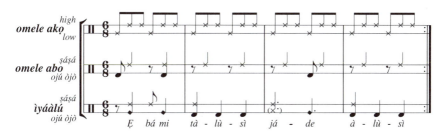

5. Whether or not the *ìyáàlù* articulates the mid and high tones on its *ojú òjò* (large skin) may also depend on rhythmic placement and/or tempo. A mid or high tone on a relatively long note value may be articulated on the *ìyáàlù's ojú òjò* (as in Ìbejì, Example 2.5, on the crotchet syllables *mú, lé* and *dé*), while a shorter note, particularly in a metrically weak position, may not be played on the *ojú òjò* but left to the *omele abo* (as in the same example, bar 6, on the quaver syllable *kẹ́*). In the cases where the *ìyáàlù* leaves out the *ojú òjò*, it may play the syllable on the *ṣáṣá* on its own, as in *kẹ́* in the example given.

Example 2.5.   The *ìyáàlù* in Ìbejì (☉ 26)

6. a. In the case of a vowel tone glide in direct speech mode, a downward tone glide from a high tone to a low tone (as in *léè* in Example 2.6) or a high tone to a mid tone (as in *Láaróyè*) is rendered by a flam from the solo *ṣáṣá* to the destination tone on the *ojú òjò* without the *ṣáṣá*. This can be within one word (as in *léè* and *Láaróyè*) or there can be a glide from one word to another where there is no consonant in between (as in *Àjàlá ìjí*).

Example 2.6.   Downward tone glides on the *ìyáàlù* in direct speech mode

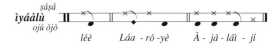

b. On occasions, both strokes on the *ojú òjò* can be left in where there is a descending tone glide, as in *oògun* in line 4 of Example 2.13, but it is more usually left out on the first syllable and rendered by the *ṣáṣá* alone, as in *tá ò* in line 6 of the same example and *bẹ̀ẹ́* in *òwe* 3 & 16, Example AII.1, ☉ 1). The *ṣáṣá* can be left in a glide in musical speech mode, most usually when the two vowels are only a tone apart (as in *leè* in Example 2.7).

Example 2.7.   Downward tone glides on the *ìyáàlù* in musical speech mode

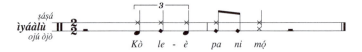

c. Flams are also employed for ascending tone glides, from the low or mid tone to a destination *ṣáṣá* stroke.

Example 2.8.   Ascending tone glide

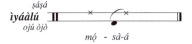

d. Vowels separated by the consonant *r* often behave as if there were no consonant and are rendered as vowel glides, although another principle is also at work (see point 13 below).

Example 2.9.   Ascending tone glide with *r*

È - jì-rẹ́

e. As I illustrate in more detail in Chapter 4, in the case of glides, an intense
vowel is usually replaced by a soft vowel in the *ẹnà* oral rendering, hence
dáa is orally rendered *hái*, instructing the drummer to leave the *ṣáṣá* out
on the second vowel. The fact that intense vowels in the second position
of a glide are often rendered without the *ṣáṣá* or by a soft vowel in *ẹnà*
corresponds with Hughes's observation that [i] and [u] often have a shorter
intrinsic duration and can be in weak metric positions. When Yorùbá
tone glides are set to music and hence gain rhythmic structure, the first
vowel of a glide is always in the strong metric position. The second vowel
also always has a lower amplitude. The second syllable is almost always
rendered without the *ṣáṣá*. There are occasional exceptions to this tendency
when the *ṣáṣá* is played on both vowels of a glide.

7. The *ìyáàlú* can, and occasionally does, play upward tone glides that start
on a low tone by striking the skin and then pressing it to create an ascending
glissando.

Example 2.10.   Ascending tone glides with *glissando*

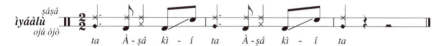

ta   À - ṣá   kì - í   ta   À -ṣá   kì - í   ta

8. While the *ṣáṣá* can articulate 'intense' vowels, it also frequently articulates
high tones without the *ojú òjò* in contexts other than tone glides as illustrated
above. Oyèlámì correctly designates solo *ṣáṣá* strokes to what he calls the
'improvizational' syllables '*lá*' and '*já*', but the syllables '*lá*' and '*já*' in actual
words are played by the solo *ṣáṣá* (hence, it is puzzling that he labels them
'improvizational').

Example 2.11.   The syllables *lá* and *já*

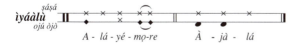

A - lá - yé - mọ-re   À - jà - lá

While '*lá*' and '*já*' (high tone only) can be played by a solo *ṣáṣá* stroke on the
ìyáàlù, there are exceptions where the high tone is also marked by a slap on the
ojú òjò (Example 2.12):

Example 2.12.   Exception on high tone *já*

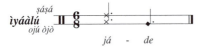

Lá and *já* are not the only syllables that are rendered by a solo *ṣáṣá*. Many other syllables can also be played by solo *ìyáàlù ṣáṣá* when one might expect a simultaneous stroke on the *ojú òjò* according to Oyèlámì's scheme. This often happens when Àyándòkun is playing *oríkì* in direct speech mode. The *oríkì* Àyàn provides a range of examples:

Example 2.13.   *Oríkì* Àyàn (☉ 2 & 12)

In the word *mẹ́rìndínlógún*, we see the *ojú òjò* strokes dropped on *mẹ́* and *ló*. *Mẹ́* glides immediately to a low tone on a soft vowel, so the juxtaposition of the *ṣáṣá* and open tone *ojú òjò* exaggerates the high-low contour. There is also no slap mute on the high tone *ló* as one would expect. As part of a single word, the *ló* in *mẹ́rìndínlógún* (sixteen) would normally be pronounced (orally and with the drum) very quickly, and three consecutive slap mutes on the *ojú òjò* up to speed may be technically difficult in this context. Three consecutive slap mutes in direct speech mode are unusual, perhaps for this reason. When I asked him, Àyándòkun agreed that often two, and always three consecutive slap mutes are technically difficult to execute at high speed, in which case the *ìyáàlù* player drops as many strokes as he can without violating the intelligibility of the drummed text. In this particular example, leaving out the slap mute on *ló* also clearly differentiates the soft-hard-soft vowel structure of *dínlógún*. Nevertheless, even when only a single slap mute is called for, it presents no technical difficulty to omit the slap mute and let the *ṣáṣá* play alone, as in *pèlé pèlé* at the end of the *oríkì*.

In line 4, there is no *ojú òjò* slap stroke on the second syllable of *iná* as the listener can easily hear the contour of the whole line *iná niyì* (MHML)[13] without it, because *á* is surrounded by the soft vowels *i*, which do not use the *ṣáṣá*.

A slap mute on a high tone is also often dropped when there is an adjacent low and high tone (as in *olójà mérìn* in line 3, *mósàá* in line 5,[14] *tònà tá ò* in line 6 and *pèlé pèlé* in line 7) or even adjacent mid tones (as in *iná niyì* in line 4), in which case the contrast of adjacent tones may be exaggerated by omitting the *ṣáṣá* to mark the lower of the two syllables. In these cases, the higher general frequency of the *ṣáṣá* mimics a rise in pitch in speech.

The *ṣáṣá* also frequently marks a syllable when surrounded by a combination of low, mid and even high tones. See *lá, lé* and *má* in Example 2.14.

Example 2.14.   The *ìyáàlù ṣáṣá* marking syllables

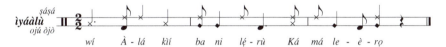

It thus appears that the *ṣáṣá* has two separate functions: (i) marking vowel intensity (as Oyèlámì illustrates); and (ii) marking high pitch (the latter not shown in Oyèlámì's scheme). Indeed, in workshop settings, Àyándòkun says that low tones are rendered by an open tone on the *ìyáàlù ṣáṣá*, mid tones are played by a mute tone on the same skin, and high tones are played by the *ìyáàlù ṣáṣá*. In this routine explanation, he usually does not mention the slap mute (at least initially) on the *ojú òjò* for a high tone. He has never explained to me (let alone introductory workshop students) how the *ṣáṣá* relates to vowels. At times, I have wondered what Àyándòkun means by 'high' when he demonstrates the tones. As well as 'high speech tone', he may well have an internalized notion of 'high volume', and even 'high intensity'.

9. The *ṣáṣá* is frequently left out when one would expect it on an intense vowel (again, violating Oyèlámì's guidelines), with the overall effect of accentuating the speech tone contour (Example 2.15). It may also depend on what comes before the relevant stroke.

---

13   Abbreviation for Mid/High/Mid/Low speech tones.

14   Àyándòkun played a mute tone on the low tone *a* in *mósàá*. Like in fast speech, there is an allowable margin of error.

Example 2.15.   *Ṣáṣá* left out on an intense vowel

The fact that many intense vowels do not always use the *ìyáàlù ṣáṣá* as expected is not random. Low-tone grammatical negative markers (low-tone *kò* or *ò*)[15] usually do not have a *ṣáṣá* stroke where one would expect it. This is because the negative marker is usually approached by a vowel glide. In the following example from *oríkì* Ṣàngó, both low-tone markers *kò* are not marked with the *ṣáṣá*, but are preceded by higher tones and therefore approached with a glide:

Example 2.16.   Negative markers

When I returned to Oyèlámì a year later with the suggestion that the *ṣáṣá* is eliminated on grammatical negative marker vowels and other descending glides, he agreed that these were two more 'rules'.[16] Nevertheless, they do appear to be optional and the negative marker *kò* occasionally includes a *ṣáṣá* stroke. The inclusion or elimination of the *ṣáṣá* depends on what actual vowel is used for the negative marker. If the negative marker is an *a*, the *ṣáṣá* is often left in. (More is explained in Chapter 4.)

10.   Yorùbá syllables containing the vowels *e*, *ẹ*, *o*, and *ọ* on any speech tones are often not marked with the *ṣáṣá*, as one would expect from viewing Oyèlámì's scheme. The *ṣáṣá* is frequently eliminated on pronouns, such as *o* (you), *ó* (he/she/it), *mo* (me), *ọ* (you as an object pronoun) and *àwọn* (them) and words beginning with *e*, *ẹ*, *o*, and *ọ*. As I explain in more detail in Chapter 4, this is because words starting with a vowel (or some consonants such as *m* and *l*) are often approached by a vowel glide, and hence the *ṣáṣá* will be left out (for example, see Example AII.1, *ọmi* in *òwe* 4 and *orí* in *òwe* 17, ☉ 1). Also, the 'softener' *o*, as in *ṣe pẹ̀lẹ́ o* and *kàwé o* in *òwe* 9 is rarely articulated with a *ṣáṣá* stroke as one would expect on an intense vowel, as it is approached by a glide.

11.   Other words containing *e*, *ẹ*, *o*, and *ọ* (not in the first position of the word) will also leave out the *ṣáṣá* (e.g. *ṣòkòtò* in ExampleAII.5, *fò* in *òwe* 10,

---

[15]   The *k* in *kò* is often truncated in spoken Yorùbá and may become part of a descending vowel glide. For example, 'we did not go' can be *a kò lọ*, *a ò lọ* or *a à lọ*, the latter rendition being a vowel glide.

[16]   I have since found a reference to negative (and other grammatical) markers in Akan drumming. See Nketia 1976:857.

jò in *òwe* 12, *kọ̀kọ̀* in *òwe* 14 and *gbò* in *òwe* 15). Again, this is because the vowels *e*, *ẹ*, *o*, and *ọ* are in between the Intrinsic Intensity extremes *i* and *u* and are therefore variable, partly due to glides, and partly because of variable split-second perceptions of the drummer. In Chapter 4, I explain more about intense Yorùbá vowels being rendered as soft *ẹnà* vowels.

12. The syllable nasals *n* and *m* are either not played at all (as in *ń* in *oríkì* Èṣù, AII.6, ☉ 6 & 16) or may be marked by a lengthened syllable (Example 2.17).

Example 2.17.   Syllabic nasals

13. The consonant *r* can be singled out from other consonants in the way it is rendered on the drum. The Yorùbá *r* is pronounced with what linguists call a 'flap', and can be represented in several ways on the drum, using what Àyándòkun sometimes refers to as 'hand rolls':[17]

      a. In two syllable words with an *r* at the beginning of the second syllable, the first syllable often has a shorter value than the second:[18]

Example 2.18.   Shortened syllables before *r* in musical speech mode

In direct speech mode, *r* is often rendered with a flam, either joining the syllable beginning with *r* to the preceding syllable (as in *hòrò hóró*, *ká rógun* and *òrìṣà*), or a flam can be added to the syllable starting with *r* (as in *okùnrin*):

---

[17]   In a discussion of the Japanese mnemonic system called *shōga,* as applied to flute traditions, Hughes (2000:97) points out that the 'flap' [r] between identical vowels marks a simple finger-flap on the flute.

[18]   I noted the stroke repetitions denoting *r* in *bàtá* drumming before reading in Nketia (1976:773), 'An impression of shortness or rapidity is generally conveyed by the presence of *r* in the sequence of nonsense syllables; the syllable before the rolled consonant is comparatively shorter than the syllable which begins with it'. However, he does not note that the vocable *r* represents the consonant *r* in the word that is being encoded. Hence his rule would be better expressed as, 'The syllable preceding a syllable that begins with *r* is comparatively shorter than the syllable that begins with it'.

Example 2.19.   The consonant *r* rendered with flams

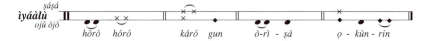

b. In two-syllable words with an *r* at the beginning of the second syllable, both syllables may be of shorter value than those surrounding them:

Example 2.20.   The consonant *r* with short syllables

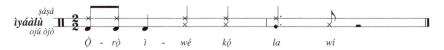

c. Sometimes an extra stroke can be added to the syllable before that beginning with *r,* or the syllable beginning with *r* (as in *orí*):

Example 2.21.   The consonant *r* rendered with repeated syllables

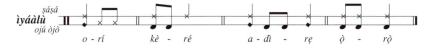

d. In words with three syllables, the syllable before that starting with *r* can either be given a relatively short note value, or the first two syllables will be relatively shorter than the third (see *òrìṣà, àràbà* and *adìrẹ* in Example 2.22). In the four-syllable word *pirigidi*, the first two syllables are relatively short.

Example 2.22.   The consonant *r* in three- and four-syllable words

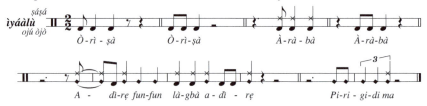

14. Although it is far less common than adding double strokes on *r*, double strokes can be added on virtually any syllable for musical effect. For example, the last syllable of the word *olódò* (custodian of the river) in *ìlù* Yemọja is repeated in various ways (see Example 2.23).

15. Many Yorùbá words are just one syllable, with most verbs being one syllable comprised of a consonant and vowel. Due to the frequent vowel-vowel juxtaposition, particularly the vowel of a verb and the first vowel of a noun, Yorùbá

Example 2.23.   Repeated syllables (☉ 27)

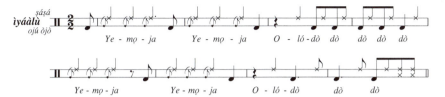

words are frequently elided. When two words are elided in the drum language, one often sees this reflected in a lengthened rhythm on the elided syllable. For example, in *àwa làgbà* (an elision of *àwa ni àgbà* in Ọ̀yọ́ dialect, or *àwa li àgbà* in Ẹ̀gbá dialect), one sees a longer note value for the elided syllable. The second word *BỌ́lọ́run* is an elision of *Bí Ọlọ́run*:

Example 2.24.   Elisions in musical speech mode

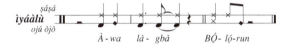

In free speech time, elided syllables are often rendered as flams. For example:

Example 2.25.   Elisions in direct speech mode

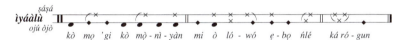

Kò mọ 'gi kò mọ̀nìyàn is an elision of *kò mọ igi kò mọ ènìyàn* (does not know trees or man). What would normally be a simultaneous mute and *ṣáṣá* tone on *mọ* becomes a flam to indicate the elision with the first syllable of *igi* (trees). *Mọ* (to know) is elided with *ènìyàn* (man), and again the simultaneous stroke on *mọ* is played as a flam to indicate the elision. *Mi ò lówó ẹbọ ńlé* is an elision of *mi ò ní owó ẹbọ ilé* (I do not have money to spare for sacrifice).[19] The elision of *ní owó* (*lówó*) is not indicated with a flam, perhaps because it is immediately followed by a tone glide from *wó* to *ẹ*. The elision of *ẹbọ ilé* is indicated by a flam on *ńlé*. The third example, *ká rógun,* is an elision of *kí a rí ogun* (to see war). The double flam (HMH) articulates the elided mid tone *a* with a flam.

16. In the *ìlù òrìṣà* there is often variation in the strokes played on any given speech tone. This is demonstrated in Example 2.26. The low tones in Ọbẹ̀dú are sometimes played by open tones on the *ìyáàlù*, and other times by a mute, while

---

19   This is taken from a different rendition of *oríkì* Ṣàngó than Example AII.5 (☉ 15).

Example 2.26.   *Ìlù* Ọbẹ̀dú (☉ 28)

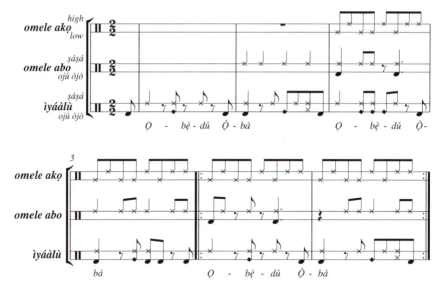

the high tone is always played by an open tone on the *omele abo*, whereas one would expect a mute.

Likewise, *Ìlù* Ọbàlùfọ̀n (Example 2.27) puts a mute on a low tone and adds numerous strokes, which partly obscure the text. Both of these examples show how musical style sometimes overrides text.

Example 2.27.   *Ìlù* Ọbàlùfọ̀n (☉ 29)

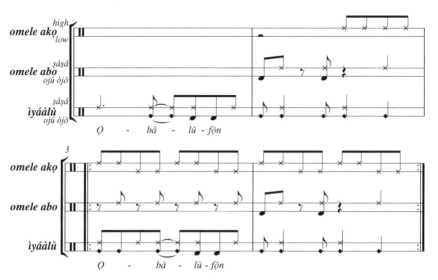

Now let us turn our attention to the second drum, which is both 'less responsible' in communicating text messages and has more options than the *ìyáàlù* in how it encodes speech.

The Omele Abo

The *omele abo* can maintain a rhythmic part while the *ìyáàlù* talks, but if the drummer knows the text, he should join in with the *ìyáàlù* as soon as he recognizes it. (As mentioned above, the *omele abo* will join in with *òwe* and *oríkì* in musical speech mode, but not with *oríkì* in direct speech mode.) Perhaps one of the reasons that the first line of an *òwe* is played more than once is to give the second drummer a chance to play along with the first line of text on the second rendering. If the *omele abo* player is very fast, he can jump in on the first line. Even when accompanying himself with a predetermined text order and a lyric sheet in front of him in the studio recordings, Àyándòkun still did not play the *omele abo* until after the entry of the *ìyáàlù*. Because he had the cue sheets, and of course is an extraordinarily skilled drummer, he usually came in during the very first line, sometimes remarkably fast (e.g., *òwe* 14), but at times he only came in on the repeat (e.g. *òwe* 3, 4, 10 and 11). As I have already stated, the *omele abo* does 'follow' the *ìyáàlù*, although only in a temporal rather than canonic or antiphonal sense. Strictly speaking, the *omele abo* accompanies the *ìyáàlù*.

Here are my findings regarding the way the *omele abo* helps the *ìyáàlù* to encode speech.

1. The first priority for the *omele abo* is to play open tones on the *ojú òjò* for mid speech tones. This creates a forefront 'melody' between the two large skins of the *ìyáàlù* and the *omele abo*. Sometimes only the two lower tones are articulated and the high tones are left out altogether. (See the *òwe* in Appendix II.)

2. The *omele abo* can play mute tones on the *ojú òjò* for high tones when it can, although these appear to be second priority and are often left out when playing at a high speed. Sometimes it can mark most high tones, as in *òwe* 1, while at other times it does not mark the high tones, as in *òwe* 13. In the latter example, the *omele abo* may drop almost all of the high tone mute strokes because it is so busy with the mid tones.

3. The *ṣáṣá* of the *omele abo* (which is not documented in Oyèlámì's text) functions in several ways:

   a. it plays non-semantic offbeat rhythmic patterns, even when its large skin is talking. In 6/8, it is often playing on the second and fifth quavers as follows (also see Example 2.4 for Ṣàngó):

Example 2.28.   *Ìlù* Ọbàtálá (☉ 30)

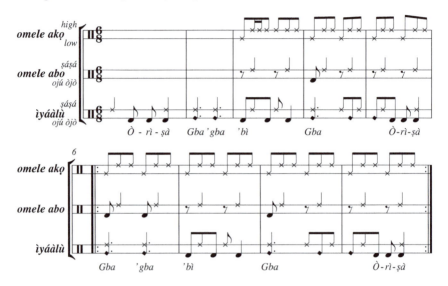

The ṣáṣá can also be more displaced, as in *ìlù* Èṣù, (Example 2.29, ☉ 31). In simple time, the *omele abo* is often playing on the quaver offbeats, as in Ọya (Example 2.3, ☉ 24).

Example 2.29.   *Ìlù* Èṣù Látọpa (☉ 31)

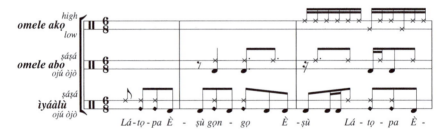

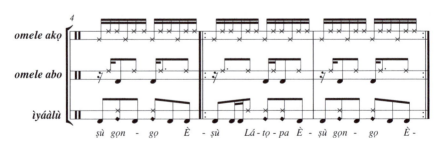

b. Further to its rhythmic function, the *omele abo ṣáṣá* can sometimes follow the rules of Intrinsic Intensity, hence functioning in a similar way to the *ìyáàlù ṣáṣá* (a function not addressed in Oyèlámì's study). Although the *ṣáṣá* often functions as a rhythmic accompaniment independent from the talking of the *ojú òjò* (as in Examples 2.28 and 2.29), its *ṣáṣá* often marks the Intrinsic Intensity of syllables on mid and high tones, particularly in passages that are rhythmically complex and fast (as in Example 2.30). In many instances, the *omele abo ṣáṣá* appears to follow the Intrinsic Intensity rules by playing with open and mute strokes on mid and high intense vowels respectively, while it rarely plays with a syllable containing *i* and *u*, unless it is fulfilling an exclusively rhythmic role. Example 2.30 illustrates the *omele abo's* sensitivity to Intrinsic Intensity in several ways. Not counting the two syllables before its entry, the *omele abo ṣáṣá* marks eight of the thirteen intense vowels while the *ṣáṣá* is absent from all of the eleven soft vowels.

c. As the *omele abo ojú òjò* does not play on low tones at all, low intense vowels are often marked by the *ṣáṣá* with nothing on the *ojú òjò,* as exemplified on the syllables *yàn kò* in bar 4 of Example 2.30. (Also see *àràbà* and Ṣàngó in Example AII.1, *òwe* 5, ☉ 1).

Example 2.30.   *Omele abo renderings of low tones with the ṣáṣá*

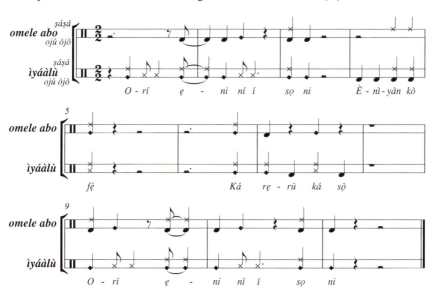

However, it rarely renders low tones of the solo *ṣáṣá* on *i* and *u*. This is particularly interesting to me as Àyándòkun often marked the low tones with touch tones[20] on the *ojú òjò* while he was teaching me the rhythms, but after analysing Àyándòkun's

---

[20]   Touch tones are also known as 'ghost tones' and are played to help keep time and create rhythmic precision in many forms of African and diasporic drumming traditions.

recorded performance, I now realize that this is a teaching device rather than a performance practice.

   d. Like the *ìyáàlù*, the *omele abo ṣáṣá* can play high tones in the absence of mute tones, as exemplified in Example 2.31 on the syllables *ló, ná, tó, ló* and *ó*. Conversely, it can also mark low tones with the *ṣáṣá*, such as on the syllables *rè* and *À* in the same example. That the *omele abo ṣáṣá* can mark both high and low tones means that the *omele abo* player may juxtapose solo *ṣáṣá* strokes to encode different speech tones, as in *rè* and *ló* in bar 1 of Example 2.31.

Example 2.31.   *Omele abo* renderings of high tones with the *ṣáṣá*

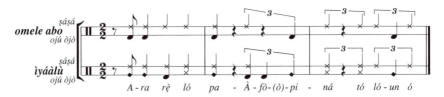

It is this ambiguity that makes the *omele abo* dependent on, and most effective when combined with, the *ìyáàlù*, while it is the *omele abo's* highlighting of mid tones that adds to the overall intelligibility of the *bàtá* ensemble.

Summary

To recapitulate the findings listed in this chapter, the *bàtá* can: (i) mimic the three tones of Yorùbá using a range of strokes and stroke combinations; (ii) mark vowel Intrinsic Intensity with the presence or absence of the *ṣáṣá*; (iii) distinguish particular syllables (*lá* and *já*) by marking them with a solo *ṣáṣá* stroke (although I do not yet know why these particular syllables are treated differently);[21] (iv) mark descending and ascending tone glides; (v) mark syllabic elisions with extended rhythmic values or flams; (vi) indicate grammar (including negative markers and pronouns) by eliminating the *ṣáṣá* where one would expect it; and (vii) differentiate the consonant *r* by employing specific hand strokes or distinctive rhythms. Points (i)–(iii) build on the findings of Oyèlámì, while points (iv)–(vii) are entirely my own. However, these seven key findings are probably far from comprehensive, as I suspect that there are numerous other techniques at work, which I have yet to recognize.

---

   [21]   I noticed several examples presented by Euba (such as 1990:235) that entirely drop the syllable *lá* when rendered on the *dùndún,* and I suspect that there may be a parallel principle at work.

By this point of the book, the reader should at least have a grip on the main speech surrogacy techniques of the *ìyáàlù* and *omele abo* within the traditional *bàtá* ensemble, along with an awareness of its fluidity and complexity. Now let us turn our attention to the *omele mẹta* and the *dùndún*, which each have their own unique methods of mimicking speech and are more easily understood by modern Yorùbá speakers.

Chapter 3

Other Voices: The *Omele Mẹ́ta* and the *Ìyáàlù Dùndún*

Chapter 2 focussed on the three-piece ensemble that Àyándòkun refers to as the 'traditional' *bàtá* group comprised of the *ìyáàlù*, the *omele abo* and the *omele akọ*. In this chapter, I discuss a recent innovation within the *bàtá* ensemble, the *omele mẹ́ta*, which is now deeply rooted in Yorùbá popular music and is widely regarded as the clearest talker of the *bàtá* ensemble. I will also describe the talking technology of the *dùndún* by drawing from the research of Euba (1990) and adding some new findings of my own. In making comparisons between the three speech surrogate methods – (i) the *ìyáàlù bàtá* and its assistant the *omele abo*; (ii) the *omele mẹ́ta*; and (iii) the *dùndún* – I will dispel the myth that the *bàtá* is a 'stammerer' that 'talks with difficulty'.

The *Omele Mẹ́ta*

The two smallest accompanying drums of the traditional *bàtá* ensemble are called the *omele akọ* and the *kúdi*. The primary difference between these two accompanying drums is that the pitch of the *kúdi* is lowered with a dark brown tuning paste called *ìda*. For most of the twentieth century, the *omele akọ* and *kúdi* have been tied together (as in plate 1.1) and played by one musician. When the two drums are attached, the *kúdi* loses its separate identity and the two-headed drum is also known as *omele akọ*. When three small accompanying drums are tied together, two of them are tuned with *ìda* (which lowers the pitch) and the three-headed drum is known as the *omele mẹ́ta* (*omele* or *emele* meaning 'accompanying drum' and *mẹ́ta* meaning 'three'). The two-headed *omele akọ* fulfils a purely rhythmic role, while the three-headed *omele mẹ́ta* can emulate the three tones of Yorùbá speech and hence is a speech surrogate instrument, whereas the *omele akọ* is not (see photograph 3.1).

When and how the *omele mẹ́ta* came into being, and who may have invented the new talking instrument, is slightly contentious. Via multiple communications since 1999, Àyándòkun has claimed to have instigated the *omele mẹ́ta* in stage performances in 1973, at which time he was one of the drummers for *jùjú*[1] artist Ahuja Bello. Àyándòkun initially used the solo *ìyáàlù* on stage with Bello, but this was not received well by Christian audiences because of the drum's unambiguous association

---

[1] *Jùjú* is a style of Yorùbá popular music that evolved in the twentieth century from eclectic sources, including church music (see Waterman 1990b).

Illustration 3.1.   The *omele mẹta*[2]

with *òrìṣà*. According to Àyándòkun, his idea for the *omele mẹta* was indirectly
inspired by Cuban congas (known in Cuba as *tumbadoras*) and their improvization
styles.[3] Africans seized upon these Cuban influences (which peaked in the 1950s),

---

[2]   This drum was made and owned by Àyándòkun. Length of each drum 23–25cm,
diameter of each drum 10–12cm.

[3]   Cuban popular music became increasingly influential in West and Central Africa as
early as the 1930s via commercial recordings and radio broadcasting. The Congo was the heart
of Latin-influenced styles and the African *rumba* recording industry. As there were thousands
of Ghanaian and Nigerian migrant workers in the Congo, much of the Cuban influence in
West Africa came via the Congo. However, Cuban music was also disseminated throughout
the region by radio and multi-national record companies (dominated by The Gramophone
Company, which later became EMI, Decca, and Philips, which later became Polygram). The
most influential recordings were the Latin American GV series released by the Gramophone
Company, Ltd. on the His Master's Voice label. Some of the most significant tracks from this
era (1928 to 1953) have been re-released on a compilation *Out of Cuba: Latin American music
takes Africa by storm* (see discography). See Roberts (1972, part 3) and Stapleton and May

creating local instruments such as the *àkúbà* drums (known as 'African congas') and recording genres of their own. Àyándòkun said that he initially had the idea to tie the three small accompanying drums together through listening to recordings of Orlando Owoh, who was a well-known exponent of 'palm wine' highlife known as 'Toye' music. Owoh originally played bongos and began using three or four congas. In highlife and *jùjú* music, it became customary for the conga player to take a 'talking' solo. When he was a child, Àyándòkun loved Owoh's music and thought that his conga playing was 'similar to *bàtá*'. Owoh was one of the pioneering musicians who used three congas to mimic Yorùbá speech. Yorùbá listeners became so accustomed to hearing the congas mimic speech that they would even read semantic meaning into a non-semantic solos.[4] Àyándòkun said he had the idea to transfer the three talking skins of the conga onto the three small talking skins of the *omele mẹ́ta*. This new talking drum was very well received by Bello's audiences, unlike Àyándòkun's earlier ventures with the *iyáàlù bàtá*. Of this period, Àyándòkun remarked, 'People loved it. When I took a solo, everybody came to spend money'. For a drummer, money largely dictates the destiny of a form.

After performing live with the *omele mẹ́ta* for five years, Àyándòkun made the first commercial recording of *omele mẹ́ta* with Bello in 1978. According to Àyándòkun's account, better-known recording artists King Sunny Adé and Ebenezer Obey copied the Bello recordings and instigated the *omele mẹ́ta* in their bands. King Sunny Adé released a track that thrust the *omele mẹ́ta* into the limelight with the drummed text, '*mo sá kéké mo mú regbó Ifá*' (I made facial marks and went into the Ifá grove). Following the popularization of the *omele mẹ́ta* by these big *jùjú* artists, a drummer from Ìséyìn called Ràsákì Àyánkọ́lá, who played with the *fújì*[5] star Kollington, imitated the biggest *jùjú* artists of the day and made the *omele mẹ́ta* famous in his first commercial recordings using the drum in the early 1980s. Kollington prided himself on being the first bandleader to use *omele mẹ́ta* with drum kit, boasting of his achievement through a song text, '*Àwa ná sáà ni, La kọ́lu bàtá lu jáasì*' [we take the credit for being the first to play the *bàtá* and the jazz drums[6] together]. The other biggest *fújì* star, Barrister, then introduced the *omele mẹ́ta* into his band. The *fújì* stars did not stop there, and from the late 1980s they began to tie even more small drums together into more elaborate clusters of four or more drums, increasing the potential for polyrhythmic and melodic figures, although when four or more drums are clustered, the *omele* ceases to 'talk'. The

---

(1987) for descriptions of the influence of Cuban music in West Africa generally and see Waterman (1990b:47, 102) for the specific influence in Nigeria.

[4]   Ẹdo musician Victor Uwaifo, who called his highlife music *akwete*, put out a track that had a non-textual solo. Yorùbá people extracted the text, '*Ṣíbí ti kán, tètè tètè fọwọ́ bùrẹsì*' [the spoon is broken, quickly eat with your hands] (personal communication, 'Túndé Adégbọlá, London, 1 August 2007).

[5]   *Fújì* music is a kind of Yorùbá popular music that evolved from Muslim musical traditions. See Euba 1990 and D. Klein 2000.

[6]   Jazz drums is an alternative term for drum kit.

omele mẹ́ta (or *omele mẹ́rin* or *márùn-ún* – four or five accompanying drums) has since become a distinctive stylistic feature of *fújì* music.

I have encountered both primary and secondary sources that pose challenges to Àyándòkun's claim as the sole originator of the *omele mẹ́ta*. Oyèlámì (personal communication, Ìrágbìjí, 3 September 1999) dates the appearance of *omele mẹ́ta* to 'within this past fifty years or so' while Thieme (1969:192) states, 'the musician playing the two small omele drums may add one more (called adahun in Ado Awaiye), and on one occasion I noted an omele drummer practicing with four small drums (the fourth was simply named omele, he said).' Also see a photograph (Fig. 19, p. 214) of the *omele mẹ́ta*, although Thieme has incorrectly labelled it as an *omele abo*. As Thieme conducted his fieldwork in Nigeria in 1964–66, this image is at least forty years old. In a recent communication (email, 18 October 2007), Thieme informed me that while he was still in Ìbàdàn in 1965, the *omele mẹ́ta* was just coming into use. He remembers a drummer who frequented the main market in Ìbàdàn who played the *omele mẹ́ta*. Of this anonymous drummer, Thieme stated, 'He "sort of" talked, using all three for three pitches. Sometimes he switched to two, with the third one used kind of like a *gúdúgúdú*. Mostly, he played alone. That is all I can report except that he was not a Master, and did not have an ensemble to my knowledge.' Àyándòkun was six or seven years old and living in Ẹ̀rìn-Ọ̀sun in 1965. Although it is possible that he later developed the *omele mẹ́ta* unaware of similar regional developments, the more likely scenario is that he was the first to use the *mẹ́ta* with a named artist in popular music, the first to make a commercial recording with it and/or that he was the drummer who developed its linguistic capacity.[7]

According to Àyándòkun, the *omele mẹ́ta* should not be used in *òrìṣà* ceremonies but should be confined to secular settings. The *omele mẹ́ta* is likely to appear in social settings such as naming ceremonies, funeral parties, weddings and other celebrations and draws its textual repertoire from *òwe*, although, according to Àyándòkun, the *omele mẹ́ta* never renders *oríkì*. As a recent and secular invention, the *omele mẹ́ta* is less restricted than the sacred *ìyáàlù* and *omele abo* and can even render profanities, much to the amusement of onlookers.

The drums are slung around the shoulders of the *alubàtá* and are played with a *bílálà* in each hand. The three top skins are called *ṣáṣá* and the bottom skins are never played. Àyándòkun plays the drums with the high tone by his left hand, the low tone by his right hand and the mid tone away from his body (as illustrated in Illustration 3.2). Àyándòkun said that the relative position of the low and mid tone drums is reversed by some drummers, but that the high tone would stay by the left

---

[7]   Klein (2000:46–7) reports that Àyándòkun has made a lesser claim of having introduced the *omele mẹ́ta* into popular music, as opposed to being the drum's originator. 'Iyaloja's compound [Àyándòkun's family] takes credit for introducing bàtá into popular music genres. In a local newspaper interview, Lamidi's brother Simiyu [Àyándòkun] spoke with pride, "Beating his chest, he related that he is the first person to introduce Bata into juju music" (*Daily Times* 1992).'

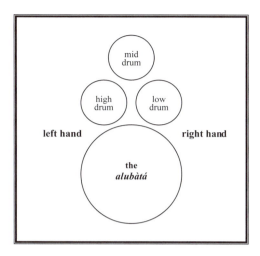

Illustration 3.2.   The playing arrangement of the *omele mẹ́ta*

hand. Àyándòkun thinks of the low tone as being equivalent to an open tone on the *ojú òjò* of the *ìyáàlù,* the mid tone drum as equivalent to the mute tone on the *ojú òjò* and the high tone as the *ṣáṣá*, hence the high tuned drum is always placed by the left hand.

The *omele mẹ́ta* is only usually used in dance rhythms such as *gbàmùn* and *ìjó oge,* and can either improvize rhythms with no semantic content or can render texts. In order to study how the *omele mẹ́ta* encodes text, I asked Àyándòkun to teach me and record the same *òwe* texts as presented in Example AII.1 and ☉ 32. Using this method, I could analyse how the *omele mẹ́ta* renders texts in comparison with the *ìyáàlù* and *omele abo* and the *dùndún.*

The *omele mẹ́ta* only renders texts in musical speech mode and to my knowledge never speaks in direct speech mode, as do the *ìyáàlù bàtá* and *dùndún.* When the *omele mẹ́ta* takes a lead role, either improvizing a non-semantic solo or rendering text, the *ìyáàlù* recedes into a supportive rhythmic role referred to as *èjìn*, and only very occasionally joins in with small segments of text. Therefore the superimposition of the *omele mẹ́ta* transcription over the *ìyáàlù* and *omele abo* transcription in Example AII.1 does not represent performance practice and has been juxtaposed purely for analytical purposes. In the recording of the *omele mẹ́ta* (☉32), it is accompanied only by the *èjìn*, which occasionally plays flourishes or joins in with the *omele abo's* speech (not notated in Example AII.1).

Comparing the *Omele Mẹ́ta's* Speech Surrogacy with the Traditional *Bàtá*

Here are my findings about how the *omele mẹ́ta* talks.

1. As a general rule, the *omele mẹ́ta* plays high speech tones on the high-tuned drum, mid speech tones on the mid-tuned drum and low speech tones on the low-tuned drum.

2. The *omele mẹ́ta* often plays a double stroke (flam), and occasionally triplets or semiquaver groups on a single syllable (see Example 3.1). The high tone in particular is frequently embellished with a flam or three- to four-note cluster on the same skin, most commonly on the intense vowels but less frequently on the soft vowels *i* and *u* (see Example 3.2). As Àyándòkun indicated and the data confirms, the high drum behaves in a similar fashion to the *ṣáṣá* of the *ìyáàlù*, obeying the Intrinsic Intensity rules. The low and mid tones may also be embellished with a simultaneous stroke on the high drum, as in Example 3.1, where the first syllable *A* in bar 1 is also embellished with a high tone.

Example 3.1.   Flams and embellishments on the high tone

3. High tones, particularly on the vowels *o* or *ọ,* are most frequently embellished with two or more strokes (see *tó* in Example 3.1 and *Bó, Ó* and *tó* in Example 3.2). The latter example also shows the less common decoration of soft vowels on *ní.*

Example 3.2.   Embellishments of *o* and *i*

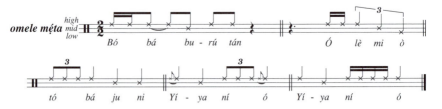

4. In the case of vowel tone glides, the *omele mẹ́ta* does not use flams like the *ìyáàlù,* but usually renders each syllable of the glide separately and rhythmically equally spaced or lengthened. In Example 3.3, the *omele mẹ́ta* lengthens the first syllable of *leè* (as in ordinary speech), whereas the *ìyáàlù* does not. The second syllable of *ọwọ́ọ̀* would sound like a flam on the *ìyáàlù* up to performance speed, while the *omele mẹ́ta* distributes the syllables evenly. Hence the *ìyáàlù* does the opposite of what happens in ordinary speech (encoding the glide) whereas the

Example 3.3.   Comparison of *omele mẹ́ta* and *ìyáàlù* tone glides

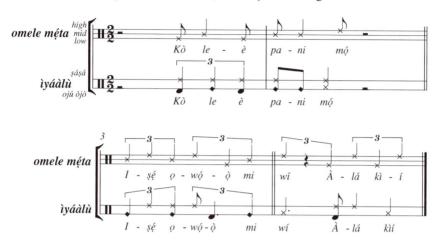

omele mẹ́ta more faithfully mimics speech pitch and rhythm. Sometimes the *omele mẹ́ta* renders a glide where the *ìyáàlù* does not (for example, *kìí* at the end of Example 3.3).

5. As with the *ìyáàlù*, the syllabic nasal *ń* is often not rendered, although there are instances where the *omele mẹ́ta* marks a nasal syllable where the *ìyáàlù* does not (see *ǹ* in Example 3.4)

Example 3.4.   Comparison of syllabic nasals on the *omele mẹ́ta* and *ìyáàlù*[8]

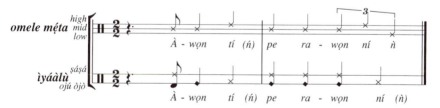

6. Where there is a consonant *r*, at least one extra stroke is added before (and less often after) the syllable starting with *r*. In Example 3.5, we see several renderings of *r*. *Òrọ̀* is played with an extra stroke before and after the *r* (notated with semiquavers) in one performance, and three strokes before the syllable beginning with *r* in another.

7. The *omele mẹ́ta* rarely leaves out or elides a syllable, and probably would only do so at extremely high speeds. Syllables which are elided by the *ìyáàlù* and *omele abo* are often 'pronounced' by the *omele mẹ́ta*. (Compare *Bí Ọlọ́run/BỌ́lọ́run*, *Àfò(ò)piná/Àfòòpiná* and *da omi/da' mi* in Example 3.6.)

_____

⁸   The *omele mẹ́ta* mid tone on the low tone syllable in the word *Àwọn* appears to be a mistake since Àyándòkun played low tones in other renderings of the word in this *òwe*.

Example 3.5.   *Omele mẹ́ta* renderings of *r*

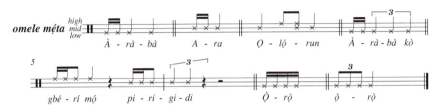

Example 3.6.   Comparison of syllable elisions on the *omele mẹ́ta* and *ìyáàlù*

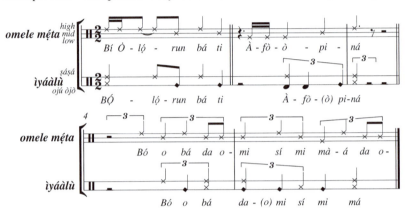

I have heard Yorùbá speakers say many times that they find the *omele mẹ́ta* easier to understand than the *ìyáàlù*. There are three reasons why the *omele mẹ́ta* is more immediately intelligible to Yorùbá speakers than the combination of the *ìyáàlù* and the *omele abo*:

a.   It is easier to perform faster notes in succession on the *omele mẹ́ta* than it is on the *ìyáàlù* and the *omele abo,* as successive *omele mẹ́ta* strokes can be played by two hands rather than one. This may largely account for why the *omele mẹ́ta* is less elided than the *ìyáàlù* and the *omele abo,* as it is easier to include all of the syllables because of the velocity of its playing technique. The fact that the *omele mẹ́ta* is less elided than the other drums may largely account for why Yorùbá listeners find it easier to understand than the traditional *bàtá;*

b.   The three speech tones are much more explicit and distinguishable on the *omele mẹ́ta* than they are on the *ìyáàlù* and *omele abo.* While the *ìyáàlù* and *omele abo* often share the low and mid tones, creating a melody, the high tone is more difficult to perceive with the slap and muted tones of the *ìyáàlù* and *omele abo* respectively. The multi-tasking function of the *ìyáàlù's ṣáṣá* may add to the difficulty of aurally eliciting the high tone. Therefore, the *omele mẹ́ta* requires less familiarity with the medium in order to hear all three tones clearly; and

c. As the *omele mẹ́ta* only draws its textual repertoire from *òwe*, which are commonly known and appropriated in ordinary speech, no specialist religious knowledge is required to understand what the drum is saying, unlike the 'traditional' *bàtá* configuration, which draws its textual repertoire from *oríkì òrìṣà* and other *òrìṣà* drum texts.

Now let us turn our attention to the *dùndún* and explore why that too is more intelligible to most Yorùbá speakers.

The *Ìyáàlù Dùndún*

Dùndún is a generic term for a family of drums. The lead drum, the subject of my research and comparison is, like the lead drum of the *bàtá* ensemble, called the *iyáàlù* (hence I label the drums with their generic terms, *dùndún* and *bàtá*, in the comparative transcriptions that follow). The supporting drums of the *dùndún* ensemble are called *kẹríkẹrì*, *ìsáájú*, *ìkẹhìn* and the *gúdúdúdú*. Apart from the *gúdúgúdú*, which is bowl-shaped with one membrane, all drums in the *dùndún* family are variable-pitch tension drums (although some of them are tied and only function as rhythmic accompanying drums). The *dùndún* is part of a larger category of hourglass-shaped, two-headed variable pitched tension drums geographically distributed as far west as Senegal and as far east as Cameroon (Thieme 1969: 12–13). Tension drums were probably introduced into Yorùbá (specifically Ọ̀yọ́) culture by their northern neighbours, the Hausa, via the spread of Islam throughout the area (Euba 1990).

The time frame for the introduction of tension drums to the Ọ̀yọ́ people is less clear, scholars designating the period from 'at least since the beginning of the sixteenth century' (Euba 1990:53), the late sixteenth century (King 1961:3), or 'only from the mid-nineteenth century on' (Kubik 1999:131).[9] Euba (51) concludes, 'Whatever the source from which the Yorùbá acquired *dùndún* there is little doubt that Ọ̀yọ́ played an important role in its diffusion within the Yorùbá territory'. Undoubtedly, the ascendance of the Ọ̀yọ́ empire in the seventeenth century was a key factor in the distribution of the drum throughout Yorùbáland. In contemporary times, the *dùndún* tradition is strongest in central and northern Yorùbáland where the Ọ̀yọ́ had the strongest influence, but the *dùndún* can be found anywhere where there are Yorùbá people.

While historical sources place the introduction of the *dùndún* into Yorùbáland between the early sixteenth century and the mid-nineteenth century, oral history

---

[9]   See Marcuzzi (2004:359–61) for a detailed challenge to Kubik's proposition of a mid-nineteenth-century introduction of the *dùndún* into Yorùbá culture, concluding that it is 'wholly untenable'.

often places its 'instigation' as coinciding with the reign of Ṣàngó, as early as the fifteenth century. Some oral histories even tie the drum to the creation myth of Odùduwà's decent in Ilé-Ifè[10] (Thieme 1969:16–17), although Thieme himself is not willing to propose a time frame, given the conflicting oral narratives he collected. According to my own research (particularly narratives from Àyándòkun), and certainly confirmed by Euba's research, the *dùndún* is a relatively recent tradition of the Yorùbá, and the *bàtá* is an older tradition. Assuming that this is historically true, then the speech surrogacy technology of the *bàtá* predates that of the *dùndún*.

There is little doubt that the *dùndún* is both more widely distributed and more popular than the *bàtá*. There are several reasons for the *dùndún's* widespread popularity. My respondents who play both *dùndún* and *bàtá* (Àyándòkun and Oyèlámì) insist that the *bàtá* is much more difficult to play than the *dùndún*, and the training of an *alubàtá* requires more time and innate ability than the training of an *aludùndún*. Therefore, it is logical that *dùndún* players are more common than *bàtá* players. Secondly, Àyándòkun's uncle, Àyángbilé (personal communication, Èrìn-Òṣun, September 2001) stated, 'All the men in the land love dancing *dùndún* and people pay more for *dùndún* than *bàtá*'. As *dùndún* rhythms are accompanied by simpler dance steps, in comparison to the more specialized and complex movements of the *bàtá's* dance, more people are able to dance to the *dùndún*, rendering it more profitable for a drummer than *bàtá* playing. As I stated in relation to the *omele mẹ́ta's* ascent in popular music, economics largely dictates the medium for a professional drummer. A third reason for the *dùndún's* wider popularity is that it is not inextricably linked with the *òrìṣà* as is the *bàtá*. The *bàtá* is historically linked with Ṣàngó's Ọ̀yọ́ kingship and the Ṣàngó *òrìṣà* cult in particular, while it is also the primary drum for the Egúngún, Èṣù and Ọya cults. Because of its unambiguous link with traditional religion, the *bàtá* has had a late and contentious entry into the church and into popular music. Even then, as exemplified by the use of *bàtá* in the band of popular music artist Lágbájá,[11] the *bàtá* does not talk much but just renders rhythm. By contrast, the *dùndún* – a more recent Yorùbá tradition and one allegedly introduced by the Hausa – does

---

[10]   The main Yorùbá creation myth is that the Yorùbá people originate from from a single ancestor called Odùduwà, who descended from heaven down to the ancient town of Ilé-Ifè. Odùduwà's descendants are said to have spread out to found their own empires. His youngest son, Ọ̀rányàn, was the mythological founder of Ọ̀yọ́. See Johnson (1976:15–25) and Ìdòwú (1994:18–29) for details of this myth. Also see Beier (1956), Law (1973) and Horton (1979) for historical analysis of and challenges to the Odùduwà/Ilé-Ifè myth.

[11]   Lágbájá was possibly the first band leader to incorporate the whole *bàtá* ensemble into popular music. When he performed for the first time in 1992 wearing his trademark mask (which evokes the Yorùbá masquerades Egúngún and *Gẹlẹdẹ́*), the twinning of the mask and the *bàtá* was evidently too strong an association with *òrìṣà* tradition for many in the audience. He was dramatically stoned off stage (personal communication, Andy Frankel, London, June 2002).

not have unambiguous associations with a particular *òrìṣà* or any traditional cult. Consequently, the *dùndún* has more easily entered Christian church services and even Muslim festivals such as *Kebir* and *Id-el-Fitr* (Euba 1990:63). The *dùndún* has also become the most common drum in secular social arenas such as naming ceremonies and weddings. In 1948, the bandleader Àkànbí Ègè pioneered the use of *dùndún* in *jùjú* music and since most of his contemporaries followed suit, the *dùndún* has long been firmly entrenched in popular music styles including *jùjú*, *fújì*, Highlife, Afrobeat and jazz (Waterman 1990b:82).

That said, the *dùndún* also plays for the *òrìṣà* and has in fact become a generic *òrìṣà* drum due to the dwindling numbers of *òrìṣà* devotees and the contracting knowledge of cult-specific drumming traditions such as the *bàtá*. If *aludùndún* know the textual repertoire, they can 'stand in' for virtually any cult-specific *òrìṣà* drummer, including the *bàtá*, *àgèrè*, *ìgbìn* and *gbẹ̀du* (Euba 1990:33–4). So, considering that the *dùndún* has a wider geographical distribution than any other Yorùbá drum and that it is used in the broadest range of contexts, including sacred, social and popular music events in Christian, Muslim and traditionalist settings, it stands to reason that the *dùndún* is the most familiar, and therefore the most intelligible, drum to modern Yorùbá speakers.

Comparing the *Ìyáàlù Dùndún's* Speech Surrogacy with the *Ìyáàlù Bàtá*

To argue the *dùndún's* intelligibility purely on a superior surrogate speech technology ignores the important factors presented above, yet one must also consider how the *dùndún* mimics speech in order to discuss why most Yorùbá speakers find it easier to understand than the *bàtá*. I have not made a dedicated study of the *dùndún* as I have the *bàtá*. Although I did make some recordings of the *dùndún* in order to compare the ways it renders the same texts in comparison to the *bàtá*, I primarily draw on the detailed research of Euba in order to make an overall comparison. While undertaking preliminary research about the *dùndún*, I have nevertheless made some interesting findings that add significant detail to Euba's research.

The *dùndún ìyáàlù* has two skins, although, unlike the *bàtá ìyáàlù*, only one skin is ever struck, and this is almost always with a curved stick with a flared end (*ọ̀pá*). The other (left) hand may be used in 'moments of excitement' (Euba 1990:143). (See Illustration 3.3.) On the smaller *dùndún* drums and the *gángan*, the drum is slung under the left shoulder of the drummer and the throngs (leather strings along the body of the drum) are tensioned using the upper arm and shoulder. The *ìyáàlù* is also slung over the left shoulder of the *aludùndún* but hangs lower by the left hip. The *ọ̀pá* is controlled by the right (or strong) hand while the left hand controls the tensioning throngs. Up to a dozen longitudinal tensioning throngs are held between the thumb and palm of the left hand and these are pushed towards the ground and slightly towards the body. Tension is also created by the throngs pressing against the left hip of the drummer. This combined movement creates a tightening

Illustration 3.3. The *ìyáàlù dùndún*[12]

of the skin and a higher-pitched note. The lowest notes are created by relaxing the left-hand tension. The *ìyáàlù's* notes have a longer decay than the *bàtá's ojú òjò*, and *glissandi* can be created by changing the throng tension with the left hand after stick impact. I have marked these *glissandi* with a line in the transcriptions.

Euba (1990:144–6) describes two main stick strokes. One is the 'free stroke', which bounces off the skin, leaving it to resonate. This stroke is primarily employed for the mid and low speech tones. The other main stroke is the 'mute stroke', where the stick stays on the skin after impact and shortens the decay of the sound. This is primarily used for high tones. Àyándòkun does not use the mute stroke described by Euba in the recordings we made, and he appears not to differentiate the speech tones with contrasting strokes (listen to ⊙ 33, 34, 35, 37). It may be that the technique described by Euba is a regional or personal style of some drummers.

---

[12]   This drum (owned by Hamish Orr) was made by Làmídì Àyánkúnlé. Length 49cm, diameter 21.5cm.

It is also possible that Àyándòkun does use this technique in actual performance but chose not to employ it in the recording sessions.

Unlike the *omele mẹ́ta*, the *dùndún* is not restricted to three absolute pitches. Rather, the *dùndún* plays three relative pitches that can shift in any moment, rather like actual speech. I have not attempted to represent or analyse these tonal shifts, but instead focus specifically on the three relative pitches, the rhythmic spacing (represented spatially in the notation of the *oríkì* in direct speech mode rather than employing rhythmic notation), *glissandi*, and at times amplitude (a choice which I will explain below). Here is a list of my findings:

1. The *dùndún* articulates all three relative speech tones, whether in direct speech mode or musical speech mode.

2. The *dùndún* usually renders vowel glides with a *glissando*. Example 3.7 provides several illustrations of how the *dùndún* and *iyáàlù* render glides with different methods.

    a. In the second line of the transcription, Àyándòkun glides down between the first two syllables of *Láaróyè*, as in speech. Then the last low tone syllable *è glissandos* upwards to represent the syllabic nasal *ń*, although there is no new stick stroke on the *ń*. The upward glide on *yò* may be a preparation for the following mid-tone syllable. The *bàtá* only represents the descending glide on the first two syllables of *Láaróyè* with a flam (shortening the syllable rather than lengthening it) and does not render *ń*.

    b. In line three of the transcription, there are explicit glides between the last low-tone syllable of *Èṣù*, the high tone *mọ́* and the low tone *ọ̀*, which has no new stick stroke. The *bàtá* only encodes the falling vowel glide in *mọ́ọ̀* with a flam, again, shortening the syllable rather than lengthening it, as in speech.

    c. To use a different example, on the word *owóò* in the second system of Example 3.10, we see an illustration of a glide in musical speech mode. Where the *bàtá* plays a short note value to depict the glide, the *dùndún* plays an elongated note value with a descending *glissando* with no new stick stroke on the destination low tone vowel.

In these and other examples, vowel glides are much more explicit and similar to ordinary speech on the *dùndún* than they are on the *bàtá*, which encodes only some of the glides with a flam, a technique which does not mimic the *glissando* of speech but rather encodes it.

3. Like the *iyáàlù bàtá*, the *dùndún* reflects the intrinsic intensity of vowels. Whereas the *bàtá* makes this explicit by playing the *ṣáṣá* on intense vowels and omitting it on the soft vowels *i* and *u*, the *dùndún* does this only with amplitude, which is a much more subtle effect. Euba (1990:198) appears to be unaware of this important performance practice. He presented four word examples with the same tone structure: *ẹbí* (family relation), *owó* (money), *iṣẹ́* (work) and *ilé* (home, house), and states, 'Since the *iyáàlù* [*dùndún*] cannot enunciate syllables, it is unable to differentiate between the above words and would render them all in the

Example 3.7.   Comparison of *oríkì* Èṣù played on the *dùndún* and *bàtá* (☉ 16
              & 33)

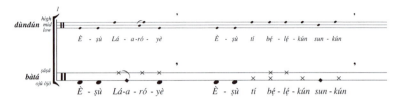

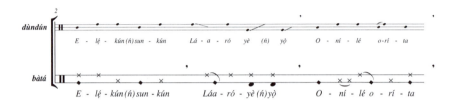

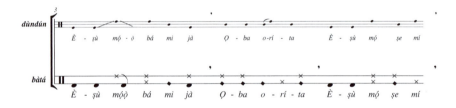

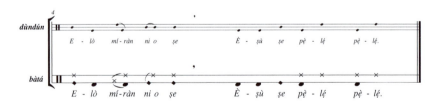

same way.' Àyándòkun has told me and demonstrated that he does differentiate
the different vowels when playing the *dùndún*, by playing soft vowels *i* and *u*
with a lower amplitude. I asked Àyándòkun to drum the same words presented as
examples by Euba (presented in the first line of Example 3.8) and I added several
other words in lines 2 and 3 to further explore the rendering of vowel Intrinsic
Intensity on the *dùndún* and the *bàtá* (☉ 35 & 36). I also added several words

to explore the rendering of *r* (more below). In the transcriptions of Àyándòkun's recorded performance in Example 3.8, I represent lower amplitudes of the soft vowels played by the *dùndún* with smaller note heads, while above the notation I have inserted amplitude graphs extracted from *Transcribe!* software. The only waveform that looks surprising is for *ọró,* which has a low amplitude on the mid-tone syllable, although this may be partly due to the flam, which requires a lighter impact so the stick can bounce.

Example 3.8.   Drummed words on the *dùndún* and *bàtá* (☉ 35 & 36)

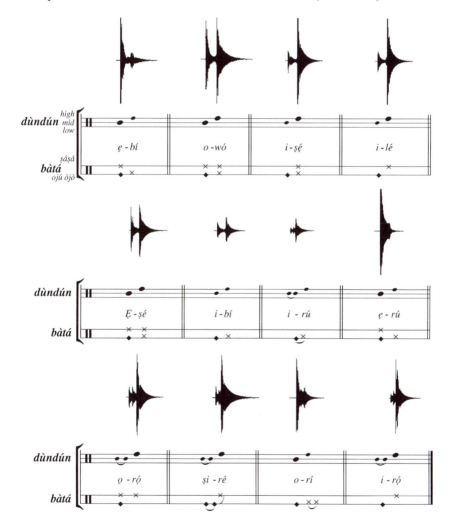

Of Euba's four example words, only *iṣẹ́* and *ilé* were drummed in the same way on the *dùndún* as they have the same soft/intense vowel structure. However, on the *bàtá* none of Euba's four example words were rendered in the same way. While the *dùndún* rendered the twelve word examples in six different ways, the *bàtá* rendered them in nine different ways. While there is significant correspondence between how the *bàtá* and *dùndún* differentiate words (illustrated in Table 3.1), the *bàtá* is more differentiated than the *dùndún*.

Table 3.1.   Coinciding word differentiations between the *dùndún* and *bàtá*

	1	2	3	4	5	6	7	8	9
dùndún	*ẹbí* *ẹrú* *orí*	*owó* *Ẹ ṣé*	*iṣẹ́* *ilé*	*ibí*	*irú*	*ọrọ́* *ṣiré* *irọ́*			
bàtá	*ẹbí* *ẹrú*	*owó* *Ẹ ṣẹ́*	*iṣẹ́*	*ibí*	*irú*	*ọrọ́*	*ilé* *irọ́*	*ṣiré*	*orí*

Euba went on to present several sentences with identical tone structures:

> *Owó layé mọ̀* (It is financial power that mankind recognizes)
> *Ayé mo júbà* (I acknowledge the importance of mankind)
> *Olá di púpọ̀* (Prestige has become manifold)
> *Iṣẹ́ ni wúrà* (Work is gold).

He correctly states that the sentences 'would be expressed with the same intonation by the *ìyáàlù* [*dùndún*] drum', although, as Example 3.9 illustrates, each sentence is played by Àyándòkun with the same intonation but contrasting amplitudes, and in the last sentence there is a double stroke on the syllable *wú*. Hence there are four different *dùndún* renderings and four different *bàtá* renderings. The *dùndún* is more differentiated, and hence a better talker than Euba realized.

4. The *dùndún* does not always play syllabic nasals, especially if a high-tone syllabic nasal follows another high-tone syllable (as in *tó ń* in the first system of Example 3.10). If it is preceded by a lower tone, the syllabic nasal is often expressed by a *glissando* without a new stick stroke, as illustrated by *Láaróyè ń yò* in line two of Example 3.7. In the same way, it can also perform a descending *glissando* to the syllabic nasal as in *ní ǹ* in the third system of Example 3.10 (both of these gliding techniques being unavailable to the *bàtá ìyáàlù* and *omele mẹ́ta*). Yet another possibility is to give the syllabic nasal its own stick stroke, as in *mò ń ṣe* in the second system of Example 3.10. Viewing the data I have collected, the *dùndún* appears to render more syllabic nasals than the *bàtá ìyáàlù*, which either

ignores them or marks them with a longer note value, as in *mò ń ṣe* in the second
system of Example 3.10.

Example 3.9.   Comparison of sentences as played by the *dùndún* and *bàtá* (⊙
                37 & 38)

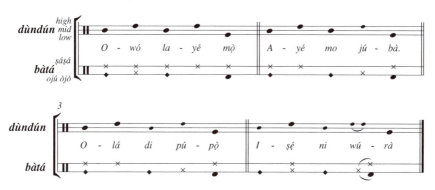

Example 3.10.   Comparison of syllabic nasals as played by the *dùndún* and *bàtá*

5. The *dùndún* renders the consonant *r* in a similar way to the *ìyáàlù* and *omele mẹta bàtá*.

    a. The consonant *r* can be represented by a shortened syllable preceding the one that begins with *r*, although in *dùndún* performance, this tends to happen only in direct speech mode and is rarely a device in musical speech mode. Example 3.11 extracts several examples from *dùndún oríkì*.

Example 3.11. *Dùndún* renderings of *r* with a shortened syllable

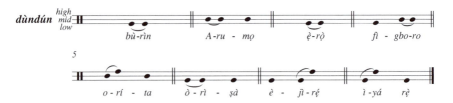

    b. Like the *ìyáàlù* and the *omele mẹta*, an extra stroke may be added to the syllable beginning with *r*, or more usually that preceding it. Both the *oríkì* and *òwe* Àyándòkun performed provide numerous examples (Example 3.12).

Example 3.12. *Dùndún* renderings of *r* with added syllables

Although there are dozens of examples of repeated syllables to represent the tongue flap *r* in Euba's transcriptions, he appears not to have recognized that most of what he refers to as 'false syllables' (230–35) (repeated strokes on one syllable) occur on a syllable that precedes a syllable beginning with *r,* or less commonly on a syllable that starts with *r*. Although he points out, 'my informants usually employed the consonant *r* when vocally interpreting false syllables', he does not indicate that syllables that begin with *r* will be represented by vocables which begin with *r*. Of the fifteen examples Euba gives in his section about 'false syllables', seven of them represent *r*, while five are vowel glides and three are elisions (*baba 'gi, ṣoba*). Therefore, what Euba refers to as 'false syllables' have semantic significance, or are not 'false' at all but rather play elided (hidden) syllables. Euba says that false syllables are 'one of the most obvious features of *dùndún*', whereas I suspect that they are one of the generic features of Yorùbá drum language across different kinds of drum ensembles.

6. Surveying the data Àyándòkun provided through his recorded performances, the *dùndún* is no more or less elided than the *ìyáàlù bàtá*, unlike the *omele mẹ́ta*, which tends to 'unpack' elided syllables. However, as Example 3.13 illustrates, the *dùndún* tends to express elisions in a different way to the *bàtá*. In this example, I have included the non-elided words in brackets under the elided ones. Neither drum indicates that *Arumọ* is an elision, but one can see two different techniques at work with *lóògùn* and *gbóògùn*. The *dùndún* appears to indicate the elision with an elongated note value (and surprisingly not a *glissando*) on both words, whereas the *bàtá* does the opposite and shortens the note value by playing a flam. In these two examples, the *dùndún* does what happens in ordinary speech and lengthens the elided syllable, whereas the *bàtá* does the opposite of what happens in speech. The *dùndún* mimics while the *bàtá* encodes. The other two elisions in Example 3.13 (*tìgbín* and *fìgboro*) are not lengthened or shortened. The first syllables of the words *lóògùn* and *gbóògùn* may be elongated because three vowels have been elided into two (rather than two into one as in the other examples).

Example 3.13.   *Oríkì* Ṣọ̀pọ̀nnọ́ as played on *bàtá* and *dùndún* (⊙ 19 & 34)

One more point worth mentioning is that the *dùndún* often renders texts more slowly than the *bàtá*. This is partly because it can, due to its sustaining facility, and partly because it needs to, due to the co-ordination required between the stick hand and the tensioning hand. The co-ordination between the left and right hands of a *ìyáàlù bàtá* player and an *omele méta* player is less complicated and faster.

A Concluding Comparison of the *Bàtá*, the *Omele Méta* and the *Dùndún*

1. The *dùndún* has several advantages that enhance its popular intelligibility:
    a. The three speech tones, as played on the *dùndún*, are uniform sounds at different pitches, whereas the *ìyáàlù bàtá* uses three different kinds of sounds (open, mute and slap/*ṣáṣá*) with the added complication of the inclusion or omission of the *ṣáṣá*, which adds to the aural complexity. If the *ìyáàlù* and *omele abo* are rendering text together, only the low and mid tones have similar kinds of sounds (the *ojú òjò* of each drum). Because of the *dùndún's* more limited range of timbres, it is much easier for the listener to identify the three speech tones immediately;
    b. The *dùndún* plays three relative pitches, which can shift in any moment, as does actual speech. The *ìyáàlù bàtá* and *omele méta* cannot do this as they are limited by the fixed tunings of each skin;
    c. The *dùndún's* technical capacity to mimic the vowel glides of ordinary speech with *glissandi* largely contributes to its intelligibility;
    d. When the *dùndún* plays a vowel glide, as well as mimicking the pitch slide with a *glissando*, it mimics the rhythm of speech, whereas the *ìyáàlù* and *omele méta* encode (rather than mimic) the glide and alter the rhythm of ordinary speech;
    e. When the *dùndún* plays syllable elisions, it mimics the rhythm of speech, whereas the *ìyáàlù* and *omele méta* encode (rather than mimic) the elision and alter the rhythm of ordinary speech;
    f. The *dùndún* appears to mimic more syllabic nasals than either the *ìyáàlù bàtá* or the *omele méta*;
    g. The *dùndún ìyáàlù* renders texts more slowly than the *ìyáàlù bàtá* and the *omele méta*, due to the mechanics of playing and the sustaining nature of the drum. It is possible that performance speed is one of the factors that makes it easier to understand the *dùndún's* surrogate speech;
    h. The *dùndún* is by far the most commonplace drum and *aludùndún* are much more numerous than *alubàtá*. The *dùndún* straddles sacred, secular and popular music domains across Christian, Muslim and traditionalist social spheres, hence modern Yorùbá speakers are most familiar with its utterances; and
    i. As the *dùndún* is not contextually limited, modern Yorùbá listeners usually do not need knowledge of traditional religious texts to understand what the drum is saying, as they do with the *bàtá's* traditional repertoire.

2. The *omele mẹta* has several advantages over the *ìyáàlù bàtá*:

   a. As with the *dùndún*, the three speech tones played on the *omele mẹta* are uniform sounds at different pitches, whereas the *ìyáàlù* uses three different kinds of sounds (described in 1. (iii) above). This uniformity of the three drum sounds makes the three speech tones easier to identify;

   b. The use of the *omele mẹta* in popular music was historically preceded by and inspired by the use of three 'talking' congas in popular music. Hence many listeners were already familiar with the medium of three heads emulating the three Yorùbá speech tones;

   c. When the *omele mẹta* plays a vowel glide, it does not alter the rhythm of ordinary speech as much as the *ìyáàlù* does by encoding glides with flams;

   d. Likewise, when the *omele mẹta* plays an elision, it does not alter the rhythm of ordinary speech as much as the *ìyáàlù* does by encoding glides with flams;

   e. The *omele mẹta* plays syllabic nasals more often than the *ìyáàlù bàtá* and the *omele abo*;

   f. Due to the two-stick technique of the *omele mẹta*, it is able to both make *r* syllables more explicit with embellishments and to 'unpack' syllables that are commonly elided in ordinary speech, on the *ìyáàlù* and the *dùndún*. This eliminates some of the ambiguity.

   g. As a new, secular invention, the *omele mẹta* is far more present in popular music (which transcends Christian, Muslim and traditionalist social spheres) than the *ìyáàlù bàtá*. Hence modern Yorùbá speakers are more familiar with the utterances of the *omele mẹta* than they are the *ìyáàlù* and *omele abo*;

   h. As the *omele mẹta* is also not contextually limited, modern Yorùbá listeners do not need knowledge of traditional religious texts to understand what the drum is saying, as they do with the traditional *bàtá* ensemble. As the *omele mẹta* primarily renders *òwe*, which are common in ordinary speech, it is easy for listeners to identify what the drum is saying.

Although the above list of advantages of the *dùndún* and *omele mẹta* may appear to weaken my argument that the traditional *bàtá* is at least as good a talker as these drums, it is not difficult to defend the remarkable surrogate speech capacity of the traditional *bàtá*.

While the *alubàtá* has a refined command of how words are rendered on the drum (be it conscious or not), it is true that most current Yorùbá speakers have problems deciphering the *bàtá's* language due to the enormous amount of possibilities and variables in its system, and a general unfamiliarity with its style of talking and its religious texts. Beier was correct when he said, 'It is much more difficult to talk on it [the *bàtá*], and far more difficult to understand it' (1954:30). Playing the *bàtá* involves more training than the *dùndún* and has an overlapping yet distinct repertoire of texts. Nevertheless, the *bàtá* does not talk 'with some difficulty being a stammerer' (Láoyè 1959:10), but rather it '*kólòlò*' (speaks in a staccato manner) with stunning mastery.

The *bàtá* can in fact do everything that the *dùndún* and *omele mẹta* can do, in respect of representing ordinary speech, yet, as I have demonstrated in the last two chapters, its methods are unique. If one is to imagine a surrogate speech continuum with encoding on one end (where one would place, say, morse code) and mimicking on the other (where one would situate synthesized speech), the traditional *bàtá* would be situated towards the encoding side, the *omele mẹta* would sit in the middle, and the *dùndún* would be situated towards the mimicking side:

encoding  **mimicking**

In viewing this model, one should consider the fact that the traditional *bàtá's* surrogate speech technology did not evolve in order to 'speak to the masses', as the *omele mẹta* and *dùndún* did over the twentieth century. The fact that the *bàtá* – once exclusively a war and cult drum – is less immediately intelligible than the more recent 'less traditional' Yorùbá drums means that the *bàtá* is still doing its job by communicating only with 'those who know', through using sounds only immediately recognizable to insiders. In modern Nigeria, 'those who know' include: (i) a diminishing group of Àyàn *bàtá* drummers themselves; (ii) the Ọ̀jẹ̀ masqueraders who intermarry with them and dance for them; (iii) their patrons, such as the kings, chiefs and other big men and women they play for and who reciprocate with cash; and (iv) the dwindling cohort of (mostly poor) devout cult insiders who also hire and 'spray' the drummers.

Beyond the limitations of human speech recognition, ideologically, the *òrìṣà* are believed to understand every *bàtá* utterance made by a master *alubàtá*. If the *òrìṣà* do not respond to *bàtá* rhythms by possessing their devotees, then religious insiders may say the *alubàtá* are not 'speaking clearly', but they would never say that the *bàtá* drum is an inadequate talker.

Chapter 4
Speaking in Codes: *Ẹnà Bàtá*

Àsọtì ló ń jẹ́ ọmọ́ gbọ́ ẹnà

[If your child understands your code language, it is because you both share the secret.][1]

As the above *òwe* indicates, Yorùbá speakers have a cultural predisposition for code-talking. This may be because – just as Yorùbá is well suited to drum language encoding due to its three-tone system – the spoken language may also be predisposed to various kinds of coding. The word *ẹnà* is a generic term for code-talking, as the Yorùbá have many different kinds of codes, including the four types described by Ìṣọ̀lá (1982), summarized below. Accordingly, the word *ẹnà* implies some form of secrecy or exclusion of certain people, such as the *ẹnà* of adults which excludes children, children's *ẹnà*, which excludes adults, hunters' *ẹnà* which is intended to exclude animals who might recognize their names, and cult insiders, such as Ifá diviners, who wish to exclude outsiders from the secrets of their rituals and medicines. However, for contemporary *alubàtá*, speaking *ẹnà* appears to be less about protecting ritual secrets and more about asserting a common lineage identity.

The *ẹnà* of *bàtá* drummers is unique in several ways. Rather than using the methods described by Ìṣọ̀lá, *ẹnà bàtá* encodes Yorùbá syllables with the vocables used to transmit strokes on the *bàtá*. All Yorùbá drumming traditions probably use vocables, but those used by *bàtá* drummers are a different set from the vocables used by, say, *dùndún* drummers, who do not have their own spoken *ẹnà*. Of all Yorùbá drummers, it is only the *alubàtá* who are known to have their own *ẹnà*. Another of the unique features of *ẹnà bàtá* is that it has a function, likely its primary function, beyond its use for conversing.

The *ẹnà* vocabulary is comprised of drum vocables, that is, non-semantic syllables that communicate drum strokes on the *bàtá*. These syllables take on semantic meaning when they are mapped from Yorùbá. As I will demonstrate in this chapter, *ẹnà bàtá* is highly efficient in communicating drum strokes orally between drummers, although *ẹnà's* semantic meaning, like drum language, is less precise than Yorùbá utterances. Nevertheless, *bàtá* drummers can extract detailed meaning from conversational *ẹnà bàtá* through contextual knowledge.

---

[1] Ìṣọ̀lá (1982:44) includes this *òwe* in his article, although Adégbọlá had told me a different version of the *òwe* to express the same idea.

One can only speculate about the origins of *ẹnà bàtá,* as I have yet to find any narratives about its instigation. One theory I propose is that *ẹnà bàtá* originated through the need for *bàtá* drummers to transmit musical information, so it initially developed as an oral notation to serve a pedagogical need.[2] If this theory is correct, then one needs to ask why *ẹnà* evolved beyond its musical function into a spoken language.

Like all Àyàn drummers, *alubàtá* have a range of rituals, including drum consecrations, where they place the *òrìṣà* Àyàn inside the drum, and initiation rites where the *òrìṣà* is 'seated' in the cranium of a devotee. *Alubàtá* may have appropriated their drum *ẹnà* for a coded ritual language as it was a 'ready-made' code and was available to adapt as a ritual language. Like Ifá diviners, the Àyàn priests could use *ẹnà* to speak in a code to exclude outsiders within earshot but outside of the ritual room.

One can only speculate, but *ẹnà's* vernacular use may have been wider than its function as a ritual language for *alubàtá.* According to oral history, the *bàtá* was the drum of the first *aláàfin* [king] of the Ọ̀yọ́ empire, Ṣàngó, who is said to have lived in the fifteenth century. The *bàtá* was also at the disposal of Ọ̀yọ́ kings descended from Ṣàngó and, according to oral literature, *bàtá* drummers would lead the Ọ̀yọ́ armies into war. The following narrative captures the partnership of Ṣàngó and Bàtá (the drum is personified in oral literature) and their war ventures:

> He [Ṣàngó] said, "I will look after everything", and Bàtá started to call all of her children.[3] Ṣàngó dashed[4] Bàtá with all of the war loot that he brought from the warfront. Bàtá said, "Lets go", and she started to chant so he could be more powerful. Ṣàngó did not rely on the traditional methods of survival, he had extraordinary powers.[5] Bàtá continued chanting war songs that kill and continued to kill. When they finished the war, Ṣàngó put his divination tray (*ìpọ̀nrí*) on the ground. He said that Bàtá should keep living with him and that they should not separate.[6]

---

[2]   I am grateful to Michael Marcuzzi for initially suggesting this theory.

[3]   '*Bàtá's* children' probably refers to the smaller accompanying *bàtá* drums.

[4]   Yorùbá English slang meaning 'gave a gift to'.

[5]   The line '*Ó ní àtàtà òràn, àtijẹ, àtimu, sánán bọlé, Ọba kòso*' is an incantation rich with metaphors and cannot be effectively captured by a direct translation. The phrase '*àtijẹ, àtimu*' translates literally as 'to survive with food and drink'. It is a metaphor that expresses the hardships people go through in order to survive. '*Sánán bọle*' is a Ṣàngó praise name which means 'putting fire into the house'. The phrase '*Ọba kòso*' is a Ṣàngó acclamation, the translation of which is contentious. There are religious and scholarly debates as to whether this means 'The king did not hang' or 'King of Kòso'. See Rouget (1965:96–7), Ìṣọ̀lá (1991) and particularly Marcuzzi (2005:247–52, 301 fn. 64) who offers a comprehensive summary and analysis of narratives.

[6]   This is a story from the *dínlógún* (cowry divining) corpus, (the sign or 'chapter' being *Ìdingbè*) as recited by Àyàngbẹ́kún, Ògbómọ̀ṣọ́, April 2002. (Transcribed and translated by Ifáfẹ́mi Awóníran.)

Reinforcing the idea of the *bàtá* as an instrument of war, a line in Àyàn's *oríkì* says, '*Ká rógun mọ́sàá niyì ọkùnrin*' [to be unafraid of war is the glory of man]. (Also see Marcuzzi 2005:162–77 for the historical context in which the *bàtá* functioned as a war drum.) If one is to assume that Ọ̀yọ́ armies fought in close proximity to the enemy, then *bàtá* drummers were on the front line within earshot of the enemy. Up to contemporary times, the *bàtá* is the primary drum of the Ṣàngó cult and indigenous devotees[7] understand the language of the drum, and hence may understand *ẹnà bàtá* to various degrees. It is therefore feasible that Ọ̀yọ́'s political and religious elite were at one time all Ṣàngó cult members and privy to *ẹnà bàtá*. If *ẹnà bàtá* was the available code to exclude outsiders, then perhaps war and the preservation of cult secrets provided the impetus for expanding its function beyond musical pedagogy.

In current Yorùbáland, *ẹnà bàtá* has several functions. Firstly, it provides an oral notation, so *alubàtá* can use *ẹnà* to educate a child (the language acquisition being one segment of the education, and the drum strokes it communicates being another). *Alubàtá* also remind one another of drum strokes during performances, whether in the context of a ritual performance or a folkloric stage performance. Ọ̀jẹ̀ masqueraders, who dance with the *bàtá*, must also understand *ẹnà bàtá* in order to perform efficiently. *Ẹnà bàtá* is also the *lingua franca* of *alubàtá* from different geographical regions. Àyándòkun says that he speaks *ẹnà* when he meets an *alubàtá* from outside his region or dialect group, in order to establish whether 'he is really a *bàtá* player'. Therefore, knowledge of the *lingua franca* functions to establish insidership and identity. *Alubàtá* can also use *ẹnà* to exclude non-speakers from the conversation. In Ọ̀yọ́ in August 2003, I had the experience of two *bàtá* drummers speaking *ẹnà* during an interview in order to exclude me, as I had a Yorùbá (though not *alubàtá*) interpreter and they also knew I could understand Yorùbá. Although I could not understand what the drummers were saying, they were immensely shocked when I identified their chat as *ẹnà bàtá*. However, they were not offended, but rather told me that they were impressed by my research skills.

Aside from actively asserting and demarcating their lineage identity, *alubàtá* also speak in *ẹnà* for amusement. Yet with the demise of *òrìṣà* devotion generally, and the Ṣàngó cult specifically, and furthermore the contraction of the traditional *bàtá* repertoire and the breakdown of former methods of musical transmission, *ẹnà bàtá* is an endangered language.

This chapter does not endeavour to present a comprehensive explanation of the *ẹnà bàtá* code, as to do so would require collecting data from several *alubàtá*, preferably from different dialectic groups. Rather, I present a study of data that I have collected from Àyándòkun between 2002 and the current time, which informs how he generates *ẹnà* from its Yorùbá source and how he matches

---

[7] I make the distinction between Yorùbá devotees and foreign Ṣàngó devotees as it is the insider knowledge of the Yorùbá language that makes an understanding of *ẹnà* possible.

vocables to drum strokes. I do not know whether his *ẹnà* system is generic to *alubàtá* without input from other drummers. This data is partly comprised of words and sentences I have collected from Àyándòkun, plus *ẹnà* recitations of the sixteen *òrìṣà oríkì* I recorded. With both the word/sentence data and the musical data, I did analyses to establish (i) which vocables match which drum strokes and (ii) what vocables can stand in for Yorùbá syllables and words. The strength of the study undoubtedly lay in the emerging model for how *ẹnà* prescribes musical performance, whereas the linguistic study of Yorùbá to *ẹnà* mapping is generally more complex and I have only undertaken a preliminary study of the relationship between Yorùbá and *ẹnà*. A deep understanding of the Yorùbá-*ẹnà* mapping requires a more concentrated project with further data collection and analysis. Essential to this process would be making recordings of more drummed text recited with *ẹnà,* plus actual conversations in *ẹnà,* rather than wholly relying on laboratory-generated data.

Adégbọlá has made a particularly important contribution to the language analysis and theoretical observations presented in the chapter. Using software he designed (see Appendix I for research methods), he has undertaken computer analysis that has corroborated my manual analyses elicited from the musical transcriptions. As a scholar of information science and linguistics, he has offered a wider insight into language perception and cognition, acoustics and information coding theory. As a native Yorùbá speaker and keen amateur musician, Adégbọlá's aural perception, which is different from my own perception as an educated musician, has also been an invaluable resource as we have listened to recordings of drumming and speech together and compared our observations.

Ẹnà Terminology and Devices

Although *ẹnà bàtá* has a unique coding system, aspects of it also relate to and borrow from other Yorùbá *ẹnà* systems. Àyándòkun has explained three different levels of *ẹnà bàtá*. His terms are: (i) 'drum language', utterances which are comprised only of the vocables that have a direct relationship to *bàtá* strokes; (ii) 'spoken *ẹnà*' or '*ẹnà* with mouth', which includes syllables and words which overlap with 'drum language' but also includes syllables not idiomatic to drum vocables; and (iii) 'broken *ẹnà*', which includes elements of (i) and (ii), but a) mixes the *ẹnà* with Yorùbá words and b) employs other *ẹnà* systems, including those reported in Ìṣọ̀lá's article. For Àyándòkun's categories to make sense to the reader, the overview presented by Ìṣọ̀lá is helpful. Ìṣọ̀lá (1982) describes four different kinds of *ẹnà* coding.

1. *The simple disordering of syllables in a word and of words in a sentence*: Ìṣọ̀lá says that this is the simplest system as nothing is added to the clear (the plain words before encoding). The example he gives is, '*Mo fẹ́ẹ́ lọ sóko*' [I want to go to the farm], which might be encoded as, '*Lọ*

móọ́ fẹ kóso'. Although the word order – and, in the case of *sóko*, the syllable order – has been scrambled, the tone structure (MHMHM) has been maintained. In this example, the subdots of *fẹ́ẹ́* stay in their original position and hence are applied to *móọ́* even though *mo* is not subdotted in the clear.

2. *The addition of null tags to syllabic unit*: a null is a meaningless syllable that is interpolated into the text to confuse the listener. The example that Ìṣọ̀lá gives from the same clear is, '*Mogo fégé logo sógó kongo*' (the null tags are underlined). In this system, the two consonants *f* and *g* may be used for the null tag, but only the latter is employed in this example. The choice of a consonant or consonants should be consistent throughout the message. The vowel has to be identical with the vowel of the preceding clear syllable. Like in (1), the tone structure is maintained. The system also marks stops and pauses by adding a syllabic nasal (in this case *ń*) before the last null, therefore *ko* becomes *kongo*. The null can also be multi-syllabic, such as *ńlolo* or *ńtiri*, so the clear becomes *Mo ńtiri fẹ́ ńtiri lọ́ńtiri sóńtiri kóńtiri*. In this second null system, the original tones of the clear have been changed.

3. *The inversion of end-of-group syllables and substitution of null tags*: in this *ẹnà* system, the nulls used are *ǹ* and *tin*. The speaker identifies a 'sense group' and the last syllable of that group is brought to the beginning of that group. The null syllable *ǹ* is prefixed to the inverted syllable, then the other null, *tin*, replaces the last syllable of the sense group. So *Bí mo bá dé* / *mo fẹ́ẹ́ lọ* / *sóko* [when I return, I want to go to the farm] becomes *ǹdè bí mo bá tín* / *ǹlọ̀ mo fẹ́ẹ́ tin* / *ǹkòsó tin*.

4. *Vowel numbers*: this system is a 'schoolboy game' that developed with the advent of literacy and encodes written forms of Yorùbá. It numbers the vowels *a* (1), *e* (2), *i* (3), *o* (4), *u* (5) and uses subdots under the numbers to denote subdotted vowels. So our clear *Mo fẹ́ẹ́ lọ sóko* becomes M4 f2̣2̣ 1ḷ s4k4 and is pronounced, '*Mà four fà* twenty-two dot *là* four dot *sà* four *kà* four'. This fourth system, which relies on orthography (and a knowledge of English, as the numbers are rendered in English) rather than phonology, is not relevant to *ẹnà bàtá*, which relies neither on a knowledge of English nor on literacy.

Drum *Ẹnà* – The Mapping of Vocables onto the *Bàtá*

In relationship to the four coding systems described by Ìṣọ̀lá, *ẹnà bàtá*, in its purest 'drum language' form, does not disorder syllables or words (although this happens in 'broken *ẹnà*'), does not add null tags (which also happens in 'broken *ẹnà*'), does not invert end-of-group syllables and has no relationship to Ìṣọ̀lá's fourth coding system, which uses a written cipher. 'Drum *ẹnà*' or 'drum language' (two terms used interchangeably by Àyándòkun) uses drum vocables to stand in for Yorùbá syllables. In order to explain the system and link it in to the speech surrogacy described in Chapter 2, I must first illustrate and explain the *bàtá's* vocables.

Ẹnà Syllables and their Drum Strokes

Example 4.1 illustrates *oríkì* Àyàn, with Àyándòkun interpolating *ẹnà* before the drummed phrases. He also recited *oríkì* Àyàn up to full speed without drumming it (☉ 40). This second *ẹnà* vocal example gives the reader an indication of what *ẹnà* sounds like when it is spoken conversationally. In the language transcription following Example 4.1, the spoken and drummed rendition (☉ 39) is on the left and oral rendition without drumming (☉ 40) is on the right. The differences between the two performances are highlighted in bold and serve as a good illustration of the variation that is typical of different renditions. There are not only differences in how Àyándòkun ordered the text phrases, but there is also some variation in consonant choices, which can be interchangeable whereas vowel choices are generally more stable.

Example 4.1.   *Oríkì* Àyàn with *ẹnà* (☉ 39)

Spoken and drummed performance (☉ 39)   **Spoken performance** (☉ 40)

*jàjàjafí jajà **fí ti**ja fí*	*jàjàjafí jajà tí fija fí*
Àyàngalú oò jí rere bí)	*(Àyàngalú oò jí rere bí)*
*jafí**di ja** jajadin*	*jafíti ṣa jajadin*
(Amúni jẹun alahun)	*(Amúni jẹun alahun)*
*jafíti ja **fi**rì fírí*	*jafíti ja tìrì fírí*
(Amúni wọ hòrò hóró)	*(Amúni wọ hòrò hóró)*
*jalájà hâì **wí**láfí*	*jalájà hâì fíláfí*
(Ọlójà mẹ̀rìn dínlógún)	*(Ọlójà mẹ̀rìn dínlógún)*

5 *jilá tidì **jaja***   *tilá tidì ṣaṣa*
   (Iná niyì ọdẹ)   *(Iná niyì ọdẹ)*

   jàjà tidì jadìdì   *jàjà tidì jadìdì*
   (Èjẹ̀ niyì oògùn)   *(Èjẹ̀ niyì oògùn)*

   fá** láti **lá ṣàá** tijì jad**ìri   *há láti hâì fá tijì jatìri*
   (Ká rógun mọ́ ṣàá jiyì ọkùnrin)   *(Ká rógun mọ́ ṣàá jiyì ọkùnrin)*

                                                   jàjàjafí ti jàlá
                                                   (Àyàngalú ṣe pẹ̀lẹ́ pẹ̀lẹ́)

                                                   kafíti jàjà hâì lá fí
                                                   (Amúni tọ̀nà táò dé rí)

10 *jàjàja**tíf i** jàlá jàlá*   *jàjàjafí ti jàlá jàlá*
   (Àyàngalú ṣe pẹ̀lẹ́ pẹ̀lẹ́)   *(Àyàngalú ṣe pẹ̀lẹ́ pẹ̀lẹ́)*

I have undertaken analyses of sixteen such drummed and spoken *oríkì*. Taking out repetitions of Yorùbá words, I collated 455 syllables and ordered the *ẹnà* and drum stroke pairing from the most frequent to the least frequent occurrences, presented in Figure 4.2. Adégbọlá used the same data source and fed the Yorùbá and *ẹnà* words into his *Prolog* software for analysis (see Appendix I for more detail). Although there was slight variation in our findings, as we arranged the raw data in slightly different ways, Adégbọlá's mechanical analysis corroborated and added to my own findings. Example 4.2 presents the actual number of occurrences of each *ẹnà* syllable and its possible stroke pairings, while recording the number of occurrences (in brackets under each syllable).

Example 4.2.   *Ẹnà* and drum stroke pairings in order of frequency

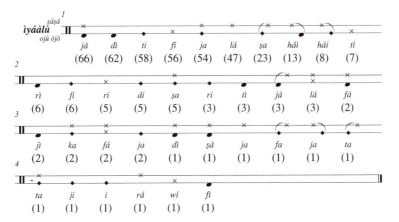

As one can see, although there is considerable variation – totalling thirty-six different syllable/drum stroke pairings – shown in Example 4.2, the data shows that these pairings are far from arbitrary. By rearranging the material into speech tone groups with vowel intensity subgroups, one can see an overriding logic even in the case of the anomalies (see Table 4.1).

As nasalized Yorùbá vowels are rarely nasalized in the *ẹnà* and do not affect the drum stoke whether or not they are nasalized, I have assimilated the rare *ẹnà* nasalized syllables into their non-nasalized equivalents (whereas Adégbọlá separated the nasalized *ẹnà* syllables, which created some variation in our data but proved insignificant in terms of the drum strokes). For example, *Lantí lantì* is coded as *janfí janfì*, though I have counted the syllables as *ja fí ja fì*. Likewise, syllabic nasals are rarely encoded in *ẹnà*. The two examples I found were *Òtòǹpòrò* in *oríkì* Ọ̀tún, which is encoded as *dìdìǹrìrì* and *bàǹtẹ́ owó* in *oríkì* Ṣàngó, which is coded with *jàháìfá*. In both cases, the syllabic nasal does not affect the drum stroke. The things that do not vary are:

1. there should never be a *ṣáṣá* stroke on the soft vowel *i* on any speech tone (the anomaly *dì* is a mistake);[8]
2. downward glides HM (*hái*) and HL (*hàì*) are always rendered in the same ways; and
3. only the vowels *a* and *i* are used.

_____

   [8] This particular anomaly appears in *oríkì* Òrìṣà Oko (see line two of Example AII.8). As I will explain in the following section on how Yorùbá is mapped onto *ẹnà*, soft *ẹnà* vowels often stand in for intense Yorùbá vowels, and the vowels *o* and *ọ* are the most common exceptions in this case scenario. As this is the only time Àyándòkun struck the *ṣáṣá* among 218 soft vowels, and there does not seem to be a feasible reason why the word *òníẹjanílé* would be exceptional, it is most likely that this is one of his rare mistakes.

Table 4.1.   *Ẹnà* and drum stoke pairings, arranged by vowel pitch and intensity

speech tone	*ẹnà* syllable	drum stroke	occurrences
low (intense vowel)	jà	open & ṣáṣá	66
		open to ṣáṣá flam	3
	fà	open & ṣáṣá	2
	ṣà	open & ṣáṣá	1
low (soft vowel)	dì	open	62
		open & ṣáṣá	1
	rì	open	6
	tì	open	3
	jì	open	2
	fì	open	1
mid (intense vowel)	ja	mute & ṣáṣá	54
		mute	2
		ṣáṣá	1
		ṣáṣá to mute flam	1
	ṣa	mute to ṣáṣá flam	23
		mute & ṣáṣá	5
	ka	mute & ṣáṣá	2
	fa	mute to ṣáṣá flam	1
	ta	mute & ṣáṣá	1
		mute to ṣáṣá flam	1
mid (soft vowel)	ti	mute	58
	fi	mute	6
	di	mute	5
	ri	mute	3
	ji	mute	1
	i	mute	1
high (intense vowel)	lá	ṣáṣá	47
		slap & ṣáṣá	3
	fá	slap & ṣáṣá	2
	rá	ṣáṣá	1
high (soft vowel)	fí	slap	56
	tí	slap	7
	rí	slap	5
	wí	slap	1
high to mid glide	hái	ṣáṣá to mute flam	8
high to low glide	hàì	ṣáṣá to open flam	13

Almost always:

1. any vocable with *i* on any speech tone prescribes a hand stroke on the large skin without with the *ṣáṣá*;
2. any vocable with *a* on any speech tone signals two simultaneous strokes or a flam, apart from *lá*; and
3. *lá* signals a solo *ṣáṣá* stroke (although there are three anomalies in the data).

An interesting fact to emerge from the data is that high speech tones are rarely played with two hands, something never explained to me by Àyándòkun and actually contradicted by Oyèlámì (1991:6). In my data, there were only five two-hand strokes out of 122 high-tone syllables (four per cent). Hence intense high *ẹnà* vowels are usually played by a solo *ṣáṣá* (thirty-nine per cent of the strokes I recorded), while soft high *ẹnà* vowels are always played by a solo slap (fifty-seven per cent of the strokes). As I recorded only one solo *ṣáṣá* stroke on the other tones (possibly a mistake), the data partially supports Àyándòkun's assertion (explained in Chapter 2) that the *ṣáṣá* is used for high tones, yet more strongly proves my own observation that the *ṣáṣá* has two functions: to differentiate the Intrinsic Intensity of vowels (supporting Oyèlámì's observation), and to mark high speech tones.

Ẹnà Consonants and their Relationship to Speech Tone

If one separates the consonants from the vowels, another data set emerges, as illustrated in Table 4.2. The consonants used (in order of frequency) are *j* (130), *t* (70), *d* (68), *f* (67), *l* (50), *ṣ* (29), *h* (21), *r* (16), *k* (2) and *w* (1), while one syllable was just *i* and was not preceded by a consonant, which is anomalous.

From listening to the recording, one can hear that Àyándòkun's pronunciation of some *ẹnà* consonants differs from his spoken Yorùbá pronunciation. While *f* is rendered more like *v* at times, *ṣ* is pronounced as fricative *sh*. In Àyándòkun's dialect (Ọ̀yọ́), both *s* as in *sun* and *ṣ* as in *shun* – which are differentiated in other Yorùbá dialects – are redacted to *s*. The *h* is very soft, and barely audible at times. In fact, as a mere three pages in the Abraham dictionary (1958) indicates, very few Yorùbá words begin with *h*. To sum up:

1. *j* is the most common consonant but never occurs on a high tone;
2. *d* mostly occurs on a low tone, occasionally on a mid tone and never on a high tone;
3. *t* mostly signals a mid tone, rarely a high tone and more rarely a low tone;
4. *f* almost always occurs on a high tone, rarely on a mid tone and more rarely on a low tone;
5. *l* only occurs on a high tone;

Table 4.2   Consonants used on the three tones

speech tone	consonant	number of occurrences
low	j	72
	d	63
	r	6
	t	3
	f	3
	ṣ	1
mid	t	60
	j	58
	ṣ	28
	f	7
	d	5
	r	3
	k	2
	i	1
high	f	57
	l	50
	t	7
	r	7
	w	1
descending glides	h	21

6. As I will illustrate in the next section, Yorùbá syllables that begin with *r* are often encoded with an *ẹnà* syllable that starts with *r*, as this is often rendered in ways specific to that consonant and therefore carries important semantic information (as described in Chapters 2 and 3);
7. *k, w* and the syllable *i* with no consonant are anomalous;
8. *ṣ* almost always occurs on a mid tone; and
9. the other Yorùbá language consonants – *b, g, gb, m, n, p, s,* and *y* – are not used in drum *ẹnà*.

As with the application of vowels to the drum, there appear to be acoustic-phonetic phenomena at work within the matching of consonants and drum strokes. Hughes (1989:3) points out, 'Frequently the choice of consonants is related to tone color, resonance and/or pitch. In drum mnemonics from many cultures, a voiced initial consonant such as *d* or *b* represents a beat on a larger drum or in the middle of the drum head, while a voiceless consonant represents a smaller drum or a stroke near the rim.' In a later article, (2000:97), he adds, 'Thus, the open bass string of Japan's *shamisen* lute is sung as [don] vs. the [ton] of the higher-pitched open middle string, and [d] represents a deeper, more resonant sound that [t] or other voiceless sounds in mnemonics for Javanese drums ([tak dung dhah]), [and] many Middle Eastern drums ([dum tek])'. As *b* is not used in *ẹnà bàtá*, *d* is used most predominantly on the bass tones (the largest head in the *bàtá* ensemble), conforming with Hughes's cross-cultural observation. Yet as I was collecting the data, Àyándòkun said that *t* and *d* can be used interchangeably 'because we find *t* and *d* in the same place'. This indicates less that *t* and *d* are interchangeable (which they are to a small degree) but, more interestingly, that Àyándòkun appears to be unconscious that he habitually divides the use of these two consonants according to relative speech tone.

Furthermore, the most common voiced consonant, *j,* never occurred on a high *ẹnà* tone within my data. The voiceless consonant *t* rarely signals a low tone, while the voiceless fricative *f* almost always signals a high tone, rarely a mid tone and even more rarely a low tone. As Hughes (2000:97) also points out, 'we find that "stop" consonants such as [p, t, k, b, d, g] generally mark the sharp attack of a plucked string or struck membranophones or idiophones'. In *bàtá* vocables, the voiceless glottal *h* always signifies a weak-to-strong hand flam, while the voiceless fricative *ṣ* usually signifies a stong-to-weak hand flam, strokes without a 'clean' or sudden beginning. In the case of *ṣa*, this vocable usually signals a flam, which indicates an elision. For example, one theory about the etymology of Yemọja (sometimes pronounced Iyemọja) is that it is an elision of *yèyé-ọmọ-ẹja* [mother of fish] although the word may be too old to be certain of the etymology. When Àyándòkun plays Yemọja, he plays three flams as follows:

Example 4.3.   Yemọja flams

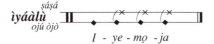

Àyándòkun has also explained to me that the position of the right hand on the large skin changes when playing a mute signalled by the *ẹnà* syllable *ṣa*. The hand moves slightly away from the rim and towards the *ìda* [tuning paste] and hits the skin with more velocity, creating a sound around a quartertone higher than an ordinary mute. He also told me several years ago that *ṣa* signals 'a hard mute with the *ṣáṣá*' and *ja* signals a 'soft mute with the *ṣáṣá*'. Like *lá*, which signifies a solo *ṣáṣá* stroke, *ṣa* has a very specific application.

Consonant and Vowel Pairing

Something that emerged from the data generated by Adégbọlá's software analysis is that: (i) certain consonants are typically combined with certain vowels; (ii) the speech tone influences the consonant/vowel combination; and (iii) some possible consonant vowel combinations are never chosen, despite the fact that they are common syllables in Yorùbá and available in *ẹnà*.

Table 4.3 illustrates which of the designated consonants are typically (or even ever) combined with the designated vowels, and on which speech tone (L, M, H) they typically, occasionally or never occur.

Table 4.3.   Consonant and vowel combinations

	a			*i*		
	L	M	H	L	M	H
d	dà	da	dá	**dì x 63**	di x 5	dí
f	fà x 2	fa x 1	fá x 2	fì x 1	fi x 6	**fì x 56**
h	hà	ha	**há x 21**	hì	hi	hí
j	**jà x 69**	**ja x 58**	já	ji x 2	ji x 1	jí
l	là	la	**lá x 50**	lì	li	lí
r	rà	ra	rá x 1	**rì x 6**	**ri x 3**	**rí x 5**
ṣ	ṣà x 1	**ṣa x 28**	ṣá	ṣì	ṣi	ṣí
t	tà	ta x 2	tá	tì x 3	**ti x 58**	tí x 7

◼ Normative *ẹnà* syllables (high number of occurrences)

▨ Anomalies/mistakes (low number of occurrences)

▢ Combinations never used on specific speech tones

▢ Combinations never used on any speech tone

While it is more difficult (and perhaps unnecessary) to explain the acoustic-phonetic reasons for why some syllables are excluded than it is to explain the syllables that are selected, one can see that reducing the number of consonant-vowel combinations adds more clarity to the vocable system. Thirty-six of the possible forty-eight combinations are used in total, yet only eleven (in the black boxes) are regularly employed. Using the current data, Table 4.4 reduces the system as far as possible. In the Yorùbá representation column, I have avoided the implication that a soft *ẹnà* vowel encodes a soft Yorùbá vowel, as there are so many exceptions to such a scheme, which I explain in the following section on the mapping of Yorùbá onto *ẹnà*.

Table 4.4.　A rudimentary scheme of ẹnà vocables

Vocable	Stroke	Yorùbá representation
dì	open	low tone soft vowel (or intense vowel exception)
jà	open & ṣáṣá	low tone intense vowel
ti	mute	mid tone soft vowel (or intense vowel exception)
ja	mute & ṣáṣá	mid tone intense vowel
fí	slap	high tone soft vowel
lá	ṣáṣá	high tone intense vowel
hái	ṣáṣá to mute flam	high to mid tone vowel glide (intense-intense or intense-soft)
hàì	ṣáṣá to open flam	high to low tone vowel glide (intense-intense or intense-soft)
rì, ri, rí *	'hand rolls'*	r + low, mid, high soft vowel
ṣa	mute to ṣáṣá flam	sometimes an elision starting on a mid tone

*　The various renderings of what Àyándòkun refers to as 'hand rolls' are described in Chapter 2.

Table 4.4 presents a useful, simplified model of how ẹnà syllables prescribe drum strokes. In order to corroborate this rudimentary scheme, one needs to work with a wider group of drummers to accrue a larger database from which more solid conclusions can be drawn. As ẹnà bàtá is a receding knowledge, and Àyándòkun neither converses in the language regularly nor uses the vocables on a regular basis, it is uncertain whether the occurrences in the low numbers (five or less) are mistakes (as in spoken language) or exceptions. It may be that the ẹnà system supports a certain number of anomalies or mistakes, and that these will be found in any up-close study of a drummer's ẹnà utterances and playing. If the strokes in low numbers are indeed exceptions and not mistakes, then one needs more data in order to elicit the nature of the exceptions. However, I am certain that the syllables *ka, i,* and *wí* do not belong in the vocable system so I did not include them in Tables 4.3 and 4.4. A likely explanation for their emergence in Àyándòkun's renditions is that they have crept in from spoken and broken *ẹnà* where these syllables regularly appear, as I will illustrate later in this chapter.

Despite the variation, fluidity and some of our unexplained data, it is nevertheless safe to conclude that neither *ẹnà* consonants nor *ẹnà* vowels – and therefore the syllables their limited combinations create – are arbitrary. The fact that *alubàtá* are probably not consciously aware of the acoustic-phonetic properties underpinning their communication system seems irrelevant, given the efficiency of *ẹnà* in prescribing specific *bàtá* drum strokes and, to a lesser extent, signifying spoken Yorùbá syllables.

The Transformation of 'Natural Language' into 'Machine Language'

Alubàtá do not directly encode Yorùbá into drum strokes. They translate Yorùbá into *ẹnà*, which is based on fewer syllables than Yorùbá, and the *ẹnà* prescribes the drum strokes.[9] So far, the discussion has centred around how *ẹnà* syllables signify drum strokes. In this section, I examine the process of translating Yorùbá into *ẹnà*.

If one considers three communication media: 1. what is uttered in Yorùbá; 2. what is uttered in *ẹnà*; and 3. what is played on the drum, the *ẹnà* mediates between spoken Yorùbá and what is drummed, as expressed by the model in Illustration 4.1, which Adégbọlá and I devised. In the centre of the circle, we have placed the term *awo,* which is usually translated into English as a noun or adjective meaning 'secret'. *Awo* can also be used as a noun to label the person who holds the secret, such as a *babaláwo* (Ifá divining priest, literally 'father of secrets'). Yet another translation of *awo* is 'esoteric knowledge' and, for our purposes, *awo* is most aptly translated as 'esoteric knowledge insider'.

The term outside of the circle, *ọ̀gbẹ̀rì,* can be translated as 'non-initiate', but for our purposes, 'esoteric knowledge outsider' serves the model. Nevertheless, as Yorùbá language and cultural insiders, *ọ̀gbẹ̀rì* are insiders on another level, which is why they are placed inside an outer dotted circle.

Skirting the arrows inside of the circle, we have placed the esoteric insiders, Àyàn, Ọ̀jẹ̀ and *olórìṣà.* Àyàn here refers to the specific segment of the lineage *alubàtá,*

---

[9]   While editing the recordings made with Àyándòkun for the CD, I noticed that when he recited *oríkì* in Yorùbá and then drummed the phrases (☉ 12–21), there were often long pauses before he drummed the phrases, whereas when he rendered the *oríkì* phrases in *ẹnà* (☉ 33, 34), there were no such pauses between what was spoken and what was drummed. I edited the long pauses out of the Yorùbá renditions whereas there was no need to do so in the fluent *ẹnà* renditions. The pauses between Àyándòkun speaking Yorùbá phrases and then drumming them may indicate that he was undergoing an extra process by 'thinking' the Yorùbá phrases in *ẹnà* before drumming them. Adégbọlá suggested that the process taking place during his pauses is akin to a computer process known as 'compilation' whereby a high-level language is broken down into machine language. Compilation is normally done by the computer, but in this case, it is a human process.

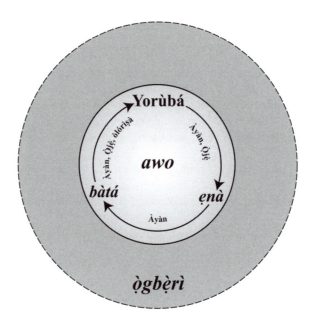

Illustration 4.1.   The Yorùbá-*ẹnà*-*bàtá* communication cycle

who have inherited and have been trained in the esoteric and practical craft of *bàtá* drumming. The model excludes other Àyàn segments such as *aludùndún,* who are not privy to *ẹnà bàtá* and would therefore be considered *ògbẹ̀rì* in this context. Òjẹ̀ refers to the craft lineage of masqueraders who constitute the Egúngún (ancestral) cult. As the *bàtá* is the drum of Egúngún, Òjẹ̀ lineage members inherit, and are trained in, the craft of carrying the mask and dancing to the *bàtá*. The Àyàn and Òjẹ̀ lineages normatively intermarry, although they are not exclusively endogamous. *Olórìṣà* is a broad term for various *òrìṣà* cult initiates. Ṣàngó, Èṣù, Ọya and Egúngún cult members most typically understand the *bàtá's* language in order to dance and conduct rituals, although members of other cults may also be conversant. Kings and chiefs were once invariably *olórìṣà*, but with cultural and religious change over the past 150 years, they are now mostly Muslims or Christians who pay allegiance to the *òrìṣà* only in key festivals. Despite their ambiguous religious status, many kings, chiefs and big men and women can still understand the language of the drum, but would not normally have access to *ẹnà*, as Òjẹ̀ lineage members do.

As the model illustrates, it is the Àyàn *alubàtá* and some Òjẹ̀ who have the exclusive knowledge of encoding Yorùbá into *ẹnà*, as presented in the top right sector of the cycle. Only the Àyàn *alubàtá,* in the lower sector of the diagram, knows how to realize the *ẹnà* as drum strokes. The top left sector, in which *bàtá* language is interpreted back into Yorùbá, is the domain of the Àyàn *alubàtá,* the Òjẹ̀ and the *olórìṣà,* who must be able to understand the drum in order to contextualize the drum's messages for dance and ritual. In fact, although beyond the bounds of this study, it is possible that *ẹnà* also functions as an indigenous dance notation as well as an oral drum notation.

The first (top right) sector of the cycle, which redacts Yorùbá into *ẹnà*, is perhaps the most complicated stage of the cycle. The transformation of *ẹnà* into drum strokes is relatively straightforward once the drummer has internalized the prescriptive scheme (oral notation) of the *ẹnà* vocables. In the top left sector of the cycle, the Yorùbá listener elicits meaning from the language of the *bàtá*. If the listener is also conversant in *ẹnà bàtá*, then he will understand what the drum is saying more easily than a mere Yorùbá speaker who is not conversant in *ẹnà* (*ògbèrì*). As Yorùbá speakers, *ògbèrì* will most likely understand some of what the *bàtá* is saying, although they will not understand to the extent of the *awo*.

Adégbọlá suggested that Illustration 4.1 has a cognate model that is applied in computer science. Adégbọlá's theoretical model of the *bàtá's* utterances as a 'machine language' (as expressed Illustration 4.2) is a viable, interdisciplinary framework that has emerged from our collaboration.

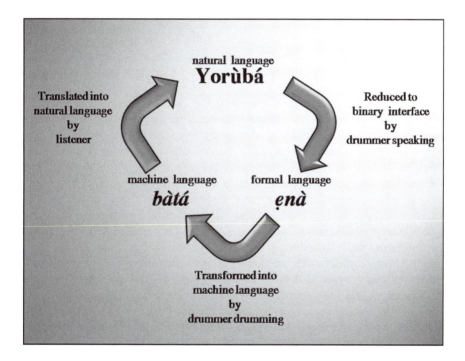

Illustration 4.2.   The transformation of natural language into machine language

In the computer science discipline, 'natural language' (or everyday human language) is spoken, written and/or signed by humans for general-purpose communication. Natural language is distinguished from 'formal language', which is used in mathematics, logic or computer science. Machine language, say from a computer or robot, is one example of machine language. As natural language is context-sensitive, human communication uses contextual cues that help to disambiguate statements made in natural language. However, machine language needs to be a lot stricter in order to obviate ambiguities. Hence, every expression in formal language should only have one meaning. The similarities between the systems of encoding human thought into drum language and into computer language are not merely symbolic. Both systems express some of the fundamental information theoretic constraints at play when man-made devices have to process human language.

There are underlying cognitive tendencies that make natural language context-sensitive. Hence, when humans need to communicate with and (sometimes) through machines, there is a need for an intermediate language that sits between natural language and machine-usable language – in other words, an interface. In computer science, this need is met by a high-level language that mediates between the natural language and the low-level machine (formal) language. This same need for an interface (that is, an intermediate language) between the natural language of Yorùbá and the machine language of the *bàtá* is met by *ẹnà*. Like the interface of computer formal language, *ẹnà* reduces Yorùbá vowels into a binary scheme.[10]

One of the important cognitive needs met by higher-level computer languages is that they provide mnemonics as memory aids to the computer programmer. Similarly, the *alubàtá* requires some memorable means of converting statements uttered in Yorùbá into drum stokes. However, because the *alubàtá* – unlike the computer programmer – is usually working in a performance mode, mere mnemonics are insufficient. *Ẹnà* therefore employs vocables which offer not only mnemonic features, but also a detailed system of oral music notation. (See footnote 8, which refers to 'compilation' in computing.

The vocabulary of *ẹnà bàtá* is comprised of vocal utterances that, through their acoustic-phonetic properties, mimic the sounds they signal on the drum (as I have explained above). The vocabulary of *bàtá* drum language consists of the sounds generated by drum strokes and their varied combinations. Even though the end product of these drum strokes may harbour some level of ambiguity for some listeners (*ọgbẹ̀rì*), there is little ambiguity between the intentions of a master *alubàtá*, the sounds that are produced and what an *awo* (*alubàtá*, Ọ̀jẹ̀ or *olórìṣà*) will hear when listening to the *bàtá*. Hence, as a *bàtá* drum statement is in a formal language, there is a one-to-one correspondence between the statement (what the *alubàtá* plays) and its realization (the sound produced and what is intelligible to *awo*).

---

10   As a talking 'machine', the *bàtá* is a binary instrument on two other levels that do not concern us here. Apart from using vocables with two vowels, which is the thrust of the binary scheme described in the main text, the drum uses two skins (*ojú òjò* and *ṣáṣá*) and talks in pairs (the *ìyáàlù* and the *omele abo*).

The Mapping of Yorùbá Language onto *Ẹnà Bàtá*

Unlike the previous section of this chapter, which only used data generated by the 16 drummed *oríkì* recorded alongside their oral *ẹnà* recitations by Àyándòkun, this section draws additionally on approximately 250 Yorùbá words that I presented to Àyándòkun either as single words or within a range of sentences. I initially prepared a questionnaire for him, which we worked through on 15 and 16 June 2002. This first questionnaire was constructed in order to collect a cross-section of vocabulary (including religious and musical terminology, everyday words and even some English loan words), a range of parts of speech (nouns, proper nouns, adjectives, verbs, pronouns, etc.), and a range of grammatical markers including negatives, past, future, continuous and plural auxiliary words). I was also mindful to collect material that included different kinds of vowel glides. Many questions and queries resulted from the analysis that emerged from the first questionnaire. I added many words and sentences to the original questionnaire, hoping to elicit missing information, and in March 2007 I undertook another interview with Àyándòkun, using the revised questionnaire. Conducting this *ẹnà* research in two blocks several years apart enabled me to ask many of the same questions, and in doing so, to establish what Àyándòkun deems to be acceptable variation. I was also able to extract new, relevant material that had not occurred to me in the initial session. Including word repetitions, the total Yorùbá word count was 1,479, which generated 1,085 *ẹnà* words. Therefore, while this data cannot necessarily support an authoritative linguistic study, it sufficiently outlines how Yorùbá is translated into *ẹnà* for the purposes of my study. Here are my findings so far.

1. The basic linguistic unit of *ẹnà* is the syllable.
2. *Ẹnà* syllables always follow the tone structure of Yorùbá.
3. *Ẹnà* words always start with a consonant. If the Yorùbá word starts with a vowel, a consonant is added – for example, *eni* becomes *jati* [person], Ẹgbé becomes Jafá [the *òrìṣà* of heavenly accomplices], *igi* becomes *fifi* [wood] and *ọta* becomes *jaja* [stone]. This is because a drum vocable needs a consonant to denote the transient of a hand stroke on the drum skin. (This is a cross-cultural property and is not exclusive to *bàtá* drumming or the Yorùbá.)
4. Yorùbá syllables containing *i* or *u* will always be rendered by an *ẹnà* syllable containing *i*, while Yorùbá syllables containing *a* will most usually be rendered by an *ẹnà* syllable containing *a* unless it is part of a glide. Yorùbá syllables containing *e*, *ẹ*, *o*, and *ọ* are usually rendered with *ẹnà* syllables containing *a,* but are sometimes rendered with *ẹnà* syllables containing *i*. To return to Hughes's model presented in Chapter 2, *a* has the highest Intrinsic Intensity of the Yorùbá vowels, while *i* has the lowest. The Yorùbá vowels in between *i* and *u* (with the lowest Intrinsic Intensity), and *a* (with the highest) are *e*, *ẹ*, *o*, and *ọ*. These intense vowels, in between the two extremes of Intrinsic Intensity, are variable. The cases of these intense vowels becoming soft vowels in *ẹnà* are so numerous that it would be misleading to state

that intense Yorùbá vowels are rendered with *ẹnà* syllables containing an *a*. However, most of the 'exceptions' – where intense Yorùbá vowels become soft *ẹnà* vowels – are coherent. Although I cannot yet explain why every exception to the soft and intense vowel mapping scheme occurs, most instances involve some kind of glide. The different glide categories I have observed are:

a. Descending glides. Where both vowels are intense in a descending vowel glide, the second vowel is rendered with *i* – for example, *dáa* [good] and *máa* [future marker] become *hái*. ('*Hái*' instructs the drummer to render the glide with a *ṣáṣá*-to-mute flam.) A high-to-low tone glide such as *bẹ́ẹ̀* [yes] becomes *hâì* in *ẹnà*. ('*Hâì*' instructs the drummer to render the glide with a *ṣáṣá*-to-open flam.) Other examples of intense vowels becoming soft are *gbáàgúdá* to *hâìfílá* and *ìyáàlù* to *dìhâìdì*. In the case where the Yorùbá contains an intense-to-soft vowel glide such as *bá mi*, the *ẹnà* is still *hái*. (Note that where *m* separates the vowels as in this example, the vowels are treated as a glide.) In a mid-to-low tone glide, the low tone can also become soft – for example, *oògùn* can become *jadìdì* [medicine]. ('*Jadì*' instruct the drummer to play a mute with the *ṣáṣá* and open tone in fast succession.) Where there are two soft vowels in a glide, such as *tìì*, a consonant is added in the second *ẹnà* syllable, which in this case is *fítì*. ('*Fítì*' instructs the drummer to play a slap and open in fast succession.)

b. Ascending vowel glides. Where there is an ascending glide on two intense vowels, the first one becomes soft – for example, Eégún becomes Tiáfí [*òrìṣà* of the ancestors] and *àlááfìà* becomes *jàdìáfíjà* [peace]. (The underlined syllables *iá/ìá* instruct the drummer to play a mute/open-to-*ṣáṣá* flam.) Sometimes both vowels in the glide become soft, such as *tòótọ́:tìílá* [truthful]. (The *ẹnà tìí* instructs the drummer to play an open and slap in fast succession.)

c. Negative markers. In Yorùbá, *kò* can be placed before a verb to denote a negative (functioning like 'not' in English). The *k* in *kò* is often truncated in spoken Yorùbá and may become part of a descending vowel glide. For example, 'we did not go' can be *a kò lọ, a ò lọ or a à lọ*, the latter rendition being a vowel glide. Therefore, in ordinary spoken Yorùbá, any vowel can be a negative marker. If the negative marker is a descending glide on Yorùbá *i*, the glide will be marked by the *ẹnà dì*, or less usually *tì* (which both prescribe an open stroke). If the negative marker is a descending glide on Yorùbá *o, ọ, e,* or *ẹ*, the glide could be marked by *dì*, or less usually *jà*, in the *ẹnà* (one- or two-handed strokes). If the glide is a descending Yorùbá *a*, it will be marked by the *ẹnà jà*, which prescribes a two-handed stroke.

d. Pronouns containing intense Yorùbá vowels are frequently rendered with soft *ẹnà* vowels. For example *o* (you), *mo* (I) and *ó* (he/she/it) are almost always rendered with *ti* or *tí*. *Ẹ* (you plural or honorific) can be rendered with *ti* or *ja*. As the pronouns *o, ó* and *Ẹ* do not start with a consonant (apart from *mo*), they will usually start with a glide from the word before, which will end with a vowel due to the consonant/vowel structure of Yorùbá. This means that when the word preceding the pronoun is on a different tone, it (the pronoun) will be approached with a glide. In the case of *mo*, I have noted in other places, mentioned in section (i), that vowels that are separated by a nasal consonant are also rendered as glides.

e. Many words that start with *e, ẹ, o* and *ọ* start with an *ẹnà* syllable containing *i*. To extract some examples from the *oríkì*, see for example Ọbàtálá (ex. App.II.7). The *ẹnà* for *Òbùnrin* is rendered in *ẹnà* as *dìdìrì* because the word preceding it is Ọbàtálá (*jajàfálá*), from which the high tone *lá* glides down to *Ò*. See also *ògúdú ègè* (*tìfì hâì dì*) in Ṣọ̀pọ̀nnọ́ (Example App.II.8). In each of these examples, the low tone on *ò* (or *è* in the second example) is preceded by a high-tone vowel so the low tone is therefore approached by a glide (*ṣáṣá*-to-open flam). Therefore a word like *oògùn* (medicine) might be rendered as *tììdì* or *jadìdì*, depending on what precedes it. Likewise, looking at my questionnaire, *ewúrẹ́* (goat) can be variously put into *ẹnà* as *jafílá* or *tifílá*, depending on whether or not the first syllable is approached with a vowel glide. In *oríkì* Ṣàngó, Ọba kòso oníbàǹtẹ́ owó becomes <u>tija</u> <u>dìti</u> <u>tifíjàhá</u> <u>tifá</u> [the king that did not hang whose skirt is adorned with cowry shells]. I have underlined the syllables where intense Yorùbá vowels become soft *ẹnà* vowels. As variation depends so much on human perception and split-second decisions, quite wide variation is sometimes available. For example, I have noted that Ògún is rendered in several ways, including Jàfí, Tìfí, Dìfí, Dìlá or Dìtí (see Example 4.3).

Example 4.4.   *Oríkì* Ògún with *ẹnà* (⊙ 41)

f. Often, it is not just the first syllable that becomes soft, such as in Òrìṣà Òkè, which becomes Dìrìjà Dìdì, and *òjò,* which is rendered as *ìdì,* in which cases the syllable that follows may dictate the *ẹnà* rendering.

5. I noted in Chapters 2 and 3 that where a syllable begins with *r,* the syllable before it is affected with a shortening or by adding a syllable. When the Yorùbá is put into *ẹnà,* the syllable preceding the one beginning with *r* frequently has an *ẹnà* syllable containing *i,* even when the source vowel was intense. This may be because *i* has a shorter Intrinsic Duration (that is, it takes less time to render orally). For example, *òrìṣà* becomes *dìdìjà* or *dìrìjá* (spiritual being), *hòrò hóró* becomes *fìrì fírí, orí* becomes *tifí* and *oríta* becomes *tiríṣa.*

6. Repeated Yorùbá syllables or patterns are often rendered with repeated *ẹnà* syllables or patterns that obey the intense/soft mapping, such as *kókóró* – *fáfárá* [key] and *fùfú* – *tìtí* [cassava meal]. However, there seem to be many exceptions where:

a. there are repeated vowels on the same tone. For example, *emele* [accompanying drum] becomes *dididi* and *gbogbo* [all] becomes *titi;*

b. three of the same vowels occur on different tones. For example, *tòlótòló* [turkey] becomes *tìlátìlá,* while *olóŋgbò*[11][cat] becomes *tiláńdì;* and

c. three different vowels on the same tone often change the intensity when put into *ẹnà.* For example, *pàtàkì* [important] becomes *ṣàdìdì* and *ehoro* [hare] becomes *titiri.*

     This may be because *alubàtá* avoid series of two-handed strokes. In the case of *tòlótòló* and *olóŋgbò,* one can see that the hand-to-hand renderings on the *bàtá* emphasize the tone contrasts. It is also possible that, like *m, n* and *r,* the liquid *l* does not separate the vowels in the same way as other consonants, and they will therefore be treated as vowel glides.

7. *Ẹnà* words of more than one syllable rarely have a Yorùbá homonym. This may be because the most prevalent syllables used in *ẹnà* are not the most prevalent in Yorùbá, and conversely, the syllables never used in *ẹnà* are the most prevalent in Yorùbá. More statistical research needs to be undertaken to prove this hypothesis.

     As there is a reduction in what consonants, vowels and consonant-vowel combinations can be used in *ẹnà,* there are undoubtedly even more homonyms in *ẹnà* than in Yorùbá. Therefore, *ẹnà* is much more context-driven than Yorùbá. As I have demonstrated with this study, an *ẹnà* word has only a limited number of possibilities in how it should be played on the *bàtá.* For example, *jaja* prescribes two strokes with a mute and the *ṣáṣá,* even though there are occasional variations, as reported in Figures 4.1 and 4.2 where four out of a total of fifty-eight strokes are slightly different. But there are many more possibilities in what the Yorùbá word *jaja* might represent. There are literally thousands of Yorùbá words containing two

---

[11] *Ológbò* is more common than *olóŋgbò.*

syllables with *a* (combined with any consonant), or even *e, ẹ, o,* or *ọ* and their multiple combinations with each other and with any consonant. Taking this isolated example into account, it is easy to see that *ẹnà* is a much more efficient system for prescribing drum strokes than it is for representing Yorùbá. That *ẹnà* is far more functional as an oral notation than as a vernacular supports the theory that *ẹnà bàtá* was originally developed as a pedagogical method for notating and teaching the *bàtá* and was appropriated as an available coded language system for other purposes.

Spoken *Ẹnà* – Expanding the Code

Àyándòkun makes a distinction between the 'drum language' described in the previous section and 'spoken *ẹnà*'. As spoken *ẹnà* has no special significance in relation to *bàtá* drum language, I have not made an extensive study of it. A concentrated study of spoken (and indeed broken) *ẹnà* would undoubtedly have more direct significance for a linguist. According to the data I have collected, the vast majority of words and phrases are the same in spoken *ẹnà* as they are in drum *ẹnà*, although there were words that Àyándòkun said can only appear in spoken *ẹnà*. Here is a summary of the examples Àyándòkun offered.

Spoken *ẹnà* employs more consonants than drum *ẹnà*. By far the most common consonant appearing in spoken *ẹnà* that does not appear in the drum *ẹnà* is *k*, which most frequently appears in *kâì* or *kái* which are used in place of the drum language *hâì* and *hái* to represent vowel tone glides. For example, *Kái tí fáfárá?* in spoken *ẹnà* (SE) is *Hái tí fáfárá?* in drum *ẹnà* (DE), *Ṣé ẹ ní kọ́kọ́ro* in Yorùbá (Y) and 'Do you have the key?' in English (E). Other words using *k* include:

> *kaka* (SE), *jaja* (DE), *ọmọ* (Y), child (E);
> *kuṣá* (SE), *tiṣá* (DE), *owó* (Y), money (E);
> *kàká* (SE), *jàjá* (DE), *bàbá* (Y), father (E);
> *kàfá* (SE), *jàfá* (DE), *ọ̀gá* (Y), one's superior (E);
> Kàfá (SE), Jàfá (DE), Ṣàngó (Y);
> Kàkàlá (SE), Jàjàlá (DE), Ṣọ̀pọ̀nnọ́ (Y);
> *korì* (SE), *ṣadì* (DE), *obì* (Y); kola nut (E).

Àyándòkun only gave isolated examples of other spoken *ẹnà* consonants that do not appear in the drum *ẹnà*:

> *g*:
> - *lágùn* (SE), *fádì* (DE), *mọ́tò* (Y), car (E);
> - *aga* (SE), *aṣọ* (Y), cloth (E), (no drum *ẹnà* given);
> *y*:
> - Yadi (SE), Ṣaṣa (DE), Ọya (Y);

m:
- *timí* (SE), *ṣafí* or *jafí* (DE), *otí* (Y), alcohol (E); and
p:
- *pẹtẹ̀* (SE), *ọbẹ̀* (Y), soup (E) (no drum *ẹnà* given);
w:
- *wari* (SE), *ẹran* (Y), meat (E) (no drum *ẹnà* given).

Broken *Ẹnà* – Mixing up the Code

According to Àyándòkun, broken *ẹnà* is a particular form of spoken *ẹnà*. He gave me many examples of words and phrases in broken *ẹnà*, totalling several hundred words. Again, as broken *ẹnà* has limited significance in relation to the drum language and the communication cycle presented in Illustration 4.2, I have not done an extensive analysis. Nevertheless, my preliminary survey shows that broken *ẹnà* both draws many of its keywords from drum *ẹnà*, and employs a range of encoding techniques drawn from well-known 'language scrambling' methods, which I summarized at the beginning of this chapter. I first became aware of broken *ẹnà* while collecting numbers, and realized that there were various and simultaneous systems of encoding at work. Table 4.5 presents three different systems of encoding. The drum *ẹnà* in the table reduces the Yorùbá syllables to drum vocables in the manner already described in this chapter. The syllable disordering uses Yorùbá, as opposed to drum *ẹnà* syllables. While the tone structure is maintained, the last vowel becomes the first vowel and *e*, *ẹ* and *ọ* become *i*. In *màárún*, the syllables are simply switched. The words in the last column use disordered syllables as the raw material, puts them on high tones, and finally adds null tags (underlined), although the treatment of 'one' is apparently different from the other numbers.

Another frequently employed device of broken *ẹnà* is combining Yorùbá and drum *ẹnà*. They can be combined in different ways, as the following two examples demonstrate (I have underlined the drum *ẹnà* keywords):

> *Gbogbo ilé ńkọ́?* (Y), *Gbogbo* <u>*tilánfá*</u>*?* (BE), How is everyone at home? (E)
> *Ìyàwó rẹ ńkó?* (Y) <u>*Tìjàlá*</u> *rẹ ńkọ́?* (BE), How is your wife? (E)

Words can be coded differently from drum language and then combined with Yorùbá. The following examples use consonants and therefore syllables that do not emerge in drum or spoken *ẹnà* (underlined):

> *Àbúrò rẹ ńkọ́?* (Y), <u>*Bàfírì*</u> *rẹ ńkọ?* (BE), How is your junior sibling? (E)
> *Ẹ̀gbọ́n rẹ ńkọ́?* (Y), <u>*Gbànmí*</u> *rẹ ńkọ́?* (BE), How is your senior sibling? (E)

Table 4.5.   Numbers in *ẹnà*

English	Yorùbá	Drum *ẹnà*	Broken *ẹnà*	
			Syllable disordering	Null tags
one	ọ̀kan	tìja	kànmi	àkan<u>hun</u>
two	méjì	lájì	jímì	no data
three	mẹ́ta	lája	támi	<u>a</u>támé<u>hun</u>
four	mẹ́rin	láji	rínmi	<u>a</u>rínmé<u>hun</u>
five	márùún	fádìí	rúnmàá	<u>a</u>rúnmá<u>hun</u>
six	mẹ́fà	jájà	fámì	<u>a</u>fámé<u>hun</u>
seven	méje	ṣája	jémi	<u>a</u>jémé<u>hun</u>
eight	méjọ	lája	jọ́mi	<u>a</u>jọ́mé<u>hun</u>
nine	mésànán	láṣàá	sánmìí	<u>a</u>sánmé<u>hun</u>
ten	méwàá	ṣáṣàá	wámìí	<u>a</u>wámé<u>hun</u>

Some sentences combine syllable disordering (underlined) and ordinary Yorùbá:

> Ọ̀rẹ́ẹ̀ mi tọ̀ọ́tọ́ (Y), <u>Rẹmîì</u> mi tọ̀ọ́tọ́ (BE), My truthful friend (E).

Others combine drum *ẹnà* (underlined) and Yorùbá:

> Ṣé àlàáfíà ni? (Y) Ṣé <u>jàdìáfíjà</u> ni? (BE), (a kind of greeting).

The following example uses drum language (*fí ti*), adds nulls (*rẹ́, hún*) and changes the tone of *wí*:

> Kí lo wí? (Y), Fí ti wirẹ́ hún? (BE), What did you say? (E).

Several different techniques can be employed simultaneously in even more ways, for example;

> Mo bá ọmọ mi nílé. (Y), I bá <u>mi</u> <u>hun</u> mọ mi <u>mi</u> ni tílá. (BE), I met my child at home (E).

In this example, there are two nulls, *mi* and *hun* (underlined). *Mo* becomes *I*, while *nílé* becomes *tílá* in drum *ẹnà*.

In summary, it appears that the broken *ẹnà* speaker has a range of devices available, and that the code is constructed in the moment in an improvizational, rather than schematic, manner – unlike drum *ẹnà* and, to a lesser extent, spoken *ẹnà,* which both have stricter schemes. Broken *ẹnà* is obviously related to *ẹnà bàtá*, as it employs so many *ẹnà bàtá* syllables and keywords. However, as so many devices are used in an apparently arbitrary manner, it seems that *ẹnà bàtá* has either been integrated into a larger *ẹnà* system, or that *ẹnà bàtá* has expanded its vocabulary and devices through a general knowledge of the larger system. As *ẹnà bàtá* is a receding knowledge and dying language, it may well be that *bàtá* drummers and Ọ̀jẹ̀ dancers have incorporated other techniques that they learned just as other Yorùbá schoolchildren learned them.

Conclusions about *Ẹnà Bàtá*

Many drumming traditions use vocables and mnemonics, but I have not heard of another system that employs drum vocables for a spoken language. That *ẹnà bàtá* derives from vocables is one of the things which distinguishes the Yorùbá *bàtá* as such a unique and remarkable tradition. Not only does the drum encode speech, but Yorùbá speakers also mimic the drum as part of a two-way process. *Ẹnà bàtá*, which harnesses acoustic-phonetic phenomena to both simplify Yorùbá into an interface and simultaneously represent the sound of the drum, is a highly efficient communicative and pedagogical system. While *ẹnà* is less efficient as a general spoken communicative system as there is so much ambiguity of meaning, it begs the question, why are *bàtá* vocables used as a language, while *dùndún* vocables (allegedly the superior surrogate speech instrument) are not? If one looks back to the conclusion of Chapter 3, I pointed out that the *dùndún* is suited to mimicking Yorùbá speech, while the *bàtá* is predisposed to encoding it. Therefore, the *dùndún* has no need for a sophisticated interface between spoken Yorùbá and drummed Yorùbá, whereas the *bàtá* requires an interface in order to make the transition into a coded 'machine language'. In fact, although Euba (1990:211–16) reports nonsense syllables and mnemonics (which are often Yorùbá texts that get mapped onto non-semantic rhythms) for the accompanying drums in the *dùndún* ensemble, no such devices are reported for the *ìyáàlù dùndún*. This is because the Yorùbá language *itself* provides the vocables for what is played on the *dùndún*.

Virtually any Yorùbá-speaking musician can pick up a *dùndún* drum and create a sound that recognizably mimics Yorùbá speech. The playing technique for the *dùndún* is sufficiently accessible that it enables a newcomer to perform a simple text slowly, although to play fast, fluently and virtuosically of course requires a high level of technique. The musicianship and knowledge threshold to be able to utter words on the *ìyáàlù bàtá* is many times higher than what is required to render text on a pressure drum, and therefore not even a seasoned *dùndún* player can pick up an *ìyáàlù bàtá* for the first time and render speech intuitively or immediately. As the *bàtá* is unlike any other Yorùbá drum (let alone African drum) and has a unique system of representing speech, which is highly coded in comparison to other Yorùbá drumming systems, this code must be *learned* at some point, and hence it also must also be *taught*. Therefore *ẹnà bàtá* is an educational device not needed in *dùndún* transmission.

As to the question of why *ẹnà bàtá* was developed beyond a pedagogy and into a vernacular, the simplest answer is that *alubàtá* communicate with *ẹnà bàtá* because they can. Not only does speaking *ẹnà* sometimes conveniently exclude outsiders, but it also establishes who is an insider [*awo*] while asserting a collective identity as Àyàn *alubàtá*. As a marginalized group, *bàtá* players are proud of the fact that their drumming tradition is difficult to access, demanding to perform and hard to penetrate. They see themselves as cultural bearers of a deep and old, albeit dying, Yorùbá tradition. The fact that they can communicate in a language only known to them and their close allies adds to their prestige and pride. *Ẹnà bàtá* is the engine in the machine, though mechanical, full of mystique – impressive and mystifying to the *ọgbẹrì*.

Epilogue
Bàtá is the Mouthpiece of *Awo*

Èyin ọmọ onílù ọmọ a fi àrán sosán
Ọmọ agbórí odó lù fún Eégún
Ọmọ agbórí odó lù fún òòṣà

[You, of the drummer lineage, who beautifies your drum with velvet stringing
Descendents of those who mount the mortar to drum for Egúngún
Descendents of those who mount the mortar to drum for *òrìṣà*][1]

Yorùbá religious outsiders (that is, those who are not traditionalists) and cultural outsiders such as myself can only hope to scratch the surface of the *bàtá's* utterances. This is perhaps my most important point in arguing against the idea that the *bàtá* is an inferior talker to the *dùndún*. That an *ògbèrì* (knowledge outsider) cannot easily elicit the text messages of the *bàtá,* while the *awo* (knowledge insider) has no trouble doing so is an indication of the *bàtá's* success and skill as a talker, not its failure. The *bàtá* uses a sophisticated coding system while the *dùndún* uses mimicry. Therefore, only those who know the *bàtá* code can easily understand its messages, while anyone who understands Yorùbá can more easily understand the *dùndún.*

While the *dùndún* is suited to speaking to *ògbèrì*, the *bàtá* is the mouthpiece of *awo*. As an *ògbèrì* instrument, the *dùndún* is ideal for speaking to the masses, which is why it has easily found its way into popular music and social settings that transcend religious alliance, educational status and class. On the other hand, the *bàtá* is still unambiguously associated with the *òrìṣà* and is therefore viewed as a relic of a backward, dark past by many contemporary Yorùbá Christians and Muslims, who would never hire a *bàtá* ensemble for their weddings, funerals or naming ceremonies, let alone their religious ceremonies. If the *bàtá* has 'difficulty speaking', it is partly because its voice is censored by contemporary Yorùbá society and partly because its ancient text messages are drowned out by popular culture and new, more accessible communication technologies.

Since completing this research project in April 2007 – by which time mobile telephones had become commonplace in Èrìn-Ọṣun – Àyándòkun installed an Internet connection in his house. As time goes on, home Internet connections may become accessible to more people in the town. While a *bàtá* text message performed by a skilled drummer can reach up to two kilometres at best, text messages generated by mobile telephones and emails demand little technical expertise, and can cross the globe in a moment. Modern communications are as novel and seductive to a

---

[1] This is the first three lines of *oríkì bàtá* collected by Táíwò Abímbọ́lá in Ọ̀yọ́, July 2007.

young Yorùbá man in Èrìn-Òṣun as the *bàtá* drum language was to me on my first visit to the town in 1999. As young Àyàn lineage members experience changing ambitions, the demands of learning to play the *bàtá* even moderately well are poorly rewarded both financially and socially. Given the allure of modern communications, the knowledge documented in this book continues to recede.

Separating Performer, Instrument and Listener

Twentieth-century composer and philosopher John Cage advocated breaking down the barriers he observed in Western art music between the composer, conductor, music performer and listener by reactivating the performer and listener out of their passive states and into active participation. He unequivocally stated, 'the division between performance and audience no longer exists' (1973:vi). *Bàtá* performance reflects Cage's holistic model whereby the separation between the 'musician' and the 'listener' is only theoretical. The *alubàtá* is the composer, conductor and performer, yet the drummers' performance is also largely directed by the people who listen, dance, chant, sing and get possessed by the *òrìṣà*. Those involved in *òrìṣà* ceremonies also theorize that the *òrìṣà* themselves, who become present in the bodies of humans, partly determine the musical performance. As the non-drummers and *òrìṣà* participate fully in the music creation process and performance drama, they may be considered musicians in their own right. In order to serve my argument, I propose an interlocking model of musician (*alubàtá*), instrument (*bàtá*) and listener (*awo/ọ̀gbẹ̀rì*) in order to draw conclusions about the *bàtá's* communication efficacy.

As a speech surrogacy instrument, the intelligibility of the *bàtá's* utterances relies on a three-tiered flow between: 1. the drummer (*alubàtá*); 2. the drum (*bàtá*); and 3. the listener (singer, dancer, possession medium).

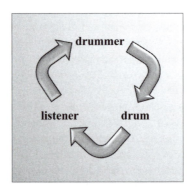

Illustration 5.1.   The three-tiered flow of information

To reiterate points made throughout this volume, in order to perform to the highest level on the *bàtá*, the musician – the *alubàtá* – needs:

1. a knowledge of the idiomatic rhythms of the *bàtá*;
2. a knowledge of Yorùbá texts, including *òwe* and *oríkì*;
3. ritual knowledge, which informs him about what rhythms and texts are appropriate in any given moment;
4. social knowledge, including background knowledge of those present, which is expressed directly through drummed *oríkì* and implied through drummed *òwe*;
5. an aesthetic sensibility that informs him about the appropriate use and the social timing of text;
6. technical know-how, enabling him to produce clear and differentiated sounds on the *bàtá*, and in turn enabling him to play and 'speak' fluently;
7. an intimate knowledge of *ẹnà*, which facilitates the transfer of Yorùbá onto the *bàtá*; and
8. a knowledge of dance, so he can respond to the lead and needs of the dancer.

As an instrument of music and speech, the *bàtá* needs to be:

1. constructed with the correct materials (wood and skin);
2. constructed with the correct dimensions and structure;
3. tuned up and in general good condition; and
4. consecrated through acceptable processes in the Àyàn lineage of the *alubàtá*.

As the one perceiving the sounds generated by the *alubàtá* and his *bàtá*, the listener needs:

1. knowledge of the Yorùbá language;
2. ritual and musical knowledge in order to recognize specific rhythms and therefore know how to dance appropriately;
3. knowledge of the *bàtá's* textual repertoire including religious *oríkì* and *òwe*; and
4. a familiarity with the way the *bàtá* renders text.

If the listener cannot understand what the drum is saying, there has been a breakdown at one or two of the three stages of the speech surrogacy process. One possibility is that the *alubàtá* is not technically proficient in playing the drum and/or is not ritually knowledgeable or well-versed in the *bàtá's* idiomatic texts. Another possibility is that the Yorùbá listener is unfamiliar with the *bàtá* and/or knows little of its idiomatic texts. A third possibility is that the *bàtá* drum is not in good working condition and the *alubàtá* is having trouble producing the right

sounds on the drum. In this last instance, it might be said that one specific *bàtá*
drum is not speaking well, but it could not be said that all *bàtá* drums are poor
talkers. If the listener cannot understand the *bàtá*, it is because either the *alubàtá*
is limited in his skill – as Àyándòkun would say, 'he does not talk clearly' – or
the listener '*kò gbọ́*' (cannot understand the language of the drum). No informed
commentator would ever say, 'the *bàtá* does not speak well'.

Láoyè's statement, 'The Iya Ilu [lead] Bàtá though suited for talking does so
with some difficulty being a stammerer' (1959:10), may be understood as the most
coherent attack on the *bàtá's* speech surrogacy capacity, as it was stated by such
an authoritative and well-respected source. As I suggested in Chapter 1, Láoyè's
statement has probably arisen from a mistranslation of the Yorùbá word *akólòlò,*
which is generally translated as 'the one who stammers'. If one interprets *akólòlò*
with another, equally viable meaning, 'one who speaks in a *staccato* manner',
then it is Láoyè's own English translation that may be problematic (as an English-
language *ògbèrì*) and not his assessment of the *bàtá's* speech surrogacy capacity.
As a Yorùbá king and serious patron of Àyàn specifically and Yorùbá traditions
generally, he was an *awo*.

Secrecy, Revelation, Ethics and the Impact of Scholarly Research

As virtuosity in speaking *ẹnà bàtá* and playing texts on the drum are both, first and
foremost, dependant on Yorùbá language fluency, the research I have documented
is highly unlikely to create a cohort of non-Yorùbá *bàtá* drummers and *ẹnà*
speakers. Furthermore, as I have yet to meet a Yorùbá drummer who can read
music, and several of my older informants have limited or no written Yorùbá
language skills or English speaking knowledge, the musical transcriptions and
their analyses will be largely inaccessible to Yorùbá drummers themselves.

The transcriptions in this volume serve a primarily analytical purpose, although
musically literate drummers in the diaspora may use them to gain access to the
bàtá repertoire, rather than use them to elucidate either the drum language or
the spoken *ẹnà*. Although I have been careful to explain that the transcriptions
and recordings are partly contrived and represent *one* particular performance of
one drummer, making them in no way definitive versions, the transcriptions and
accompanying recordings may nevertheless be understood and appropriated more
narrowly. If this volume becomes a hymn book-like resource for *aficionados* – as
the Amira/Cornelius book of Cuban *bàtá* transcriptions has to some[2] – this would
be an unfortunate misrepresentation and misunderstanding of our project.

---

[2]   Apart from some *bàtá* transcriptions in Ortiz's publications (1951, 1993 [1950]),
the Amira/Cornelius book (1991) was the first prescriptive book of transcriptions of the *oro
seco*, an instrumental segment of the Cuban *bàtá* repertoire. Amira and Cornelius were also
careful to explain that the transcriptions should not be understood as definitive.

It is the recordings with this volume (and others like them) that will likely have more impact within Nigeria than the text and transcriptions. In Àyándòkun's view, recordings are an extremely important resource for future preservation and transmission, as he fears a time when it will become increasingly difficult to sustain the traditional Àyàn pedagogy involving childhood apprenticeship and musical transmission via ẹnà bàtá. Àyándòkun regards the recordings as a contingency, as they can be passed on to young drummers after the most knowledgeable elders have died. The possibility that recordings may completely replace ẹnà as a medium of transmission was not a possibility Àyándòkun and I ever discussed. However, it is doubtful that the mere existence of bàtá and ẹnà recordings would be the cause of the breakdown or disappearance of the existing ẹnà pedagogy. Rather, recordings may fill the vacuum of receding performance and ẹnà knowledge created by modernization and changing lifestyles.

Coda

In comparing the bàtá and dùndún, Beier (1954:30) correctly stated, 'It is much more difficult to talk on it [bàtá], and far more difficult to understand it'. This is because the dùndún is an instrument suited to communicating with ògbèrì, while the bàtá is an instrument that developed a code in order to communicate with awo and exclude ògbèrì. Therefore, my conclusion (contentious and bold, considering that I am a cultural outsider) is that anybody who states that the bàtá cannot speak clearly or is an inferior talker to the dùndún must be an ògbèrì – a knowledge outsider.

APPENDICES

Appendix I
Research Methods

The Musical Data

My first *bàtá* lesson was with Múráínà Oyèlámì in June 1998, during one of his trips to London. He gave me a copy of his 1991 book. After his departure, I made Western stave transcriptions from Oyèlámì's TUBS notation and discovered numerous irregularities in the model that he proposed. In July 1999, I travelled to Nigeria for the first time and visited Oyelámì in Ìrágbìjí. We had discussions about these irregularities and I also interviewed him formally.

On this same trip, I instigated research relationships with several other *bàtá* drummers, including Àyángbémiga Àyánwálé in Ọ̀yọ́, and Rábíù Àyándòkun in Èrìn-Ọ̀sun. With these *bàtá* masters, I videoed performances, recorded lessons, which I began transcribing, and I conducted interviews, which included questions about the drum language. Over the next four field trips to Nigeria (July–September 1999, July–September 2000, August–September 2001, April 2002 and August–September 2003) I forged research relationships with more drummers, including the late Àlàbí Kébgéiyale Ọ̀súníyì Àdìgún Àyángbékún in Ògbómọ̀sọ́. I also worked with Àyántúndé Sàlàkọ́ and his group in Ṣàgámù, where they play a very different style of *bàtá* to the Ọ̀yọ́-style drummers with whom I had been working.

My research sessions with Èrìn-Ọ̀sun drummer Àyándòkun have continued sporadically up to the current time, both in Nigeria and in the UK, where he has become a frequent visitor. In my research sessions with Àyándòkun in the UK, I collected *bàtá* rhythms and *oríkì* by making audio recordings and videoing his hand strokes. I made musical transcriptions of the rhythms and texts he taught me, which generated many deepening questions. The principles that Àyándòkun had explained to me in formal lessons often contradicted the 'rules' Oyèlámí had laid out in his 1991 text, despite the fact that Àyándòkun was one of Oyèlámí's informants. My ongoing questions to Àyándòkun often revolved around these differences in performance practice and analysis.

During my AHRC fellowship at SOAS, I brought Àyándòkun to the UK as my first research collaborator. After clarifying much of the material, I took him into the SOAS studio, where I produced *bàtá* recordings of rhythms, proverbs and *oríkì*, along with some out-of-context words and sentences, which I carefully planned to elicit specific pieces of information. Together, Àyándòkun and I planned the material to match the particular renderings of the drum texts as he taught them in our lessons and as I had transcribed them. This set up a controlled recording, as a master drummer such as Àyándòkun would never normally perform texts and rhythms in exactly the same way twice. The texts in particular are usually fluid and, in a normal performance situation, a Yorùbá master drummer (playing any kind of drum) strings together fragments of an internalized repertoire of texts. How texts are constructed in performance depends on both the drummer's inspiration and aesthetic judgment in the moment, which is led by the objective needs of a ritual or a social event. Breaking with this normative performance practice, Àyándòkun sat in the studio wearing headphones with a music stand in front of him with printed texts planned in our preparatory sessions. This was quite challenging for Àyándòkun, and he inevitably made small deviations from the 'scores' in the process. In another break from performance practice, I asked Àyándòkun to overdub voice-overs of the texts, to help the listener to follow the scores and drummed texts. These recordings with the voice-over also helped me in the transcription process.

While Àyándòkun recorded, I sat to his right with a video camera and filmed his right hand on the main 'speaking' skin, the *ojú òjò*. I moved around a little to film the detailed movements of his technique. Making these video recordings gave me the opportunity both to extract the parts from the composite rhythms and to study the subtle hand movements employed. I also dubbed audio recordings, which extracted the parts for transcription purposes.

I began the transcription process while Àyándòkun was still in London so I could bring my queries to him and clarify the texts, and at times I asked him to play what was on the recordings. We also listened to most of the recordings and he helped me work through the texts and their occasional deviations from the printed 'scores' that had guided him in the studio. I converted the recordings into MP3 files and used the software *Transcribe!*, which enables one to isolate and loop segments and slow them down to fifty per cent and twenty-five per cent speed without changing the pitch. The visual representations (graphic waveforms and pitching) within the program were also useful in the transcription process. All transcriptions were done on Sibelius version four software.

Finally, I exported the hard disk audio onto Pro Tools (a digital audio workstation) and then edited and mastered it with the patient and skilled assistance of sound engineer Michel Massimino.

Ẹnà

I began collecting *ẹnà* words and sentences from Àyándòkun during one of his London visits in early 2002. I also collected some data from Lagos-based Àyánkójọ Jimọh Àyánwọlá in a London interview. As I have no formal linguistic training, I devised methods of my own in isolation. I put the *ẹnà* data I had collected into a chart and proceeded with various methods of manual analysis, such as isolating each syllable and then noting the most common transformations of Yorùbá vowels and consonants to *ẹnà* vowels and consonants. I made a list of the apparent exceptions to the emerging patterns and rules and noticed coherence of the 'exceptions'.

After compiling a formative analysis, I then questioned Àyándòkun again in 2007 using the same word and sentence list, along with a new list that was designed to address specific queries. I noted the frequent variations from his original interview, which gave me an insight into what kinds of variations are allowable.

After transcribing the sixteen drummed *oríkì* and fifteen *òrìṣà* rhythms I recorded, I then asked Àyándòkun to recite the *ẹnà* for each text, which elicited more data. I also asked him to give me these *ẹnà* texts at different moments in time, which enabled me to see what varied.

As I began to get a grip on the rules of how *ẹnà* prescribes drum strokes and how it is mapped from Yorùbá, I began attempting to use *ẹnà* to communicate with Àyándòkun while he was residing and working in my house during March and April 2007. He patiently gave me feedback, letting me know when I had spoken accurately and correcting me when I did not.

I began the *ẹnà* analysis by extracting syllables from the sixteen *oríkì* transcriptions and manually cataloguing what Yorùbá syllables they derived from and what drum strokes they prescribed. I compiled a statistical analysis and began to catalogue the emerging patterns. Adégbọlá then applied a computer programme written in *Prolog* to the same data I had analysed manually. *Prolog* is a computer language that is applied mostly to solving Artificial Intelligence problems, and so it is well suited to the analysis of language in text. While most computer programming languages are designed to deal mainly with numbers, *Prolog* is one of the very few that is designed to manipulate symbols (such as those employed for text) rather than numbers.

The Yorùbá *oríkì*, their *ẹnà* codes and the corresponding drum strokes were organized as 'terms' (facts) in a *Prolog* database. A *Prolog* 'query' (a statement that runs through all the facts in the *Prolog* database) term was employed to build a list of all Yorùbá-*ẹnà* syllable pairs in the *oríkì* database. The list of Yorùbá-*ẹnà* syllable pairs was sorted alphabetically using the *ẹnà* syllables as the sorting key. Duplicate pairs were counted and all occurrences of each *ẹnà* code were clustered. This provided information on the occurrence frequency of each *ẹnà* code and the corresponding Yorùbá syllables to which they map.

Another *Prolog* query locates all the occurrence positions of any particular Yorùbá-*ẹnà* syllable pair within the *oríkì* texts. This made it possible to examine the various contexts of each Yorùbá-*ẹnà* syllable pair. It was therefore relatively easy to recognize the core Yorùbá-*ẹnà* mapping rules, the commonalities among certain identified exceptions and the possibility of human errors in some of the exceptions without commonalities.

Text Translations

Translations of drum texts were undertaken in several stages. Àyándòkun gave me rough translations of the texts as he taught me the rhythms. I typed these up and passed them on to Adégbọlá, who then drafted more refined translations. I also cross-referenced these with secondary sources and at times rang religious experts in Nigeria to clarify archaic words. As the last step in the process, Adégbọlá and I discussed each translation in order to agree on the final versions presented in Appendix II.

Appendix II
Musical Transcriptions
and Text Translations

Òwe

AII.1. Òwe played by *bàtá ensemble* (☉ 3) & *omele mẹta*

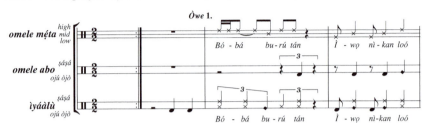

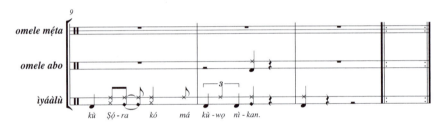

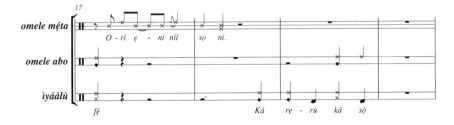

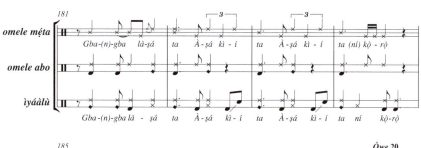

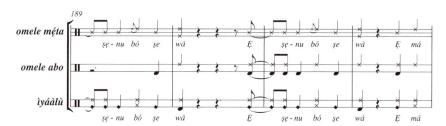

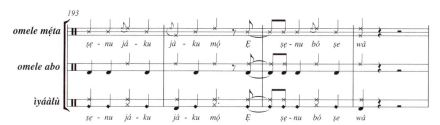

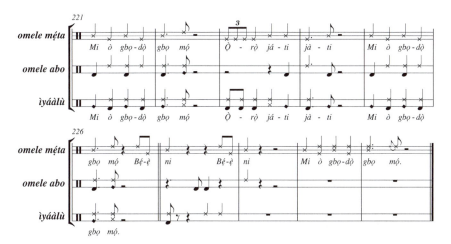

Òwe **Translations**

1.

Bóbá burú tán	When things come to a head
Ìwọ nìkan loó kù	You will be on your own
Yókùwọ nìkan	Isolated and lonely
Bó bá burú tán	When things come to a head
Ìwọ nìkan loó kù	You will be on your own
Ṣọ́ra, kó má kùwọ nìkan	Be careful not to isolate yourself
Bó bá burú tán	When things come to a head
Ìwọ nìkan loó kù.	You will be on your own.

2.

Orí ẹni níí sọ ni	It is one's *orí* (personal destiny) that averts danger
Ènìyàn kò fẹ́, ká rẹrù ká sọ̀	Most people do not wish that one succeeds
Orí ẹni níí sọ ni.	But it is one's *orí* that averts danger.

3.

Kò leè pani mọ́ (x2)	They become ineffectual in inflicting harm (x2)
BỌ́lọ́run bá tì fọ̀tá eni han ni	Those enemies that God has helped one to identify
Kò leè pa ni mọ́	They become ineffectual in inflicting harm
Bẹ́ẹ̀ ni.	That is for sure.

4.

Omi ọmọ ni o dà (x2)	Bless me with children (x2)
Bó o bá dami sí mi	If you pour water (children, wealth, curses) on me
Màá dami sí ọ	I will pour water on you[1]
Omi ọmọ ni o dà.	Bless me with children.

5.

Yíya ní ó ya	It will be ripped
Àràbà tó fojú di Ṣàngó	The *àràbà* (silk cotton tree) that dares Ṣàngó
Yíya ní ó ya.	Will be ripped.

6.

Ara rẹ̀ ní ó pa (x2)	It is destined for failure (x2)
Àfòòpiná, tó lóun ó pa fìtílà	The moth[2] attempts to extinguish an oil lamp flame[3]
Ara rẹ̀ ní ó pa.	It is destined for failure.

7.

Kò gbàgbé ẹnìkan	He abandons no one
Ọlọ́run ọba	Ọlọ́run, the great king
Kò gbàgbé ẹnìkan.	He abandons no one.

---

[1] This is a metaphor for 'Whatever your intentions towards me, I will respond with those same intentions'.

[2] Translator's note: The word *àfòòpiná* is an elision of the sentence *a fò pa iná* – 'one who flies to kill the fire' – and is a metaphor for one who is undertaking a suicide mission.

[3] Translator's note: *Fìtíla* is an open-flame oil lamp that turns out to be challenging for a moth because of the hot oil in which the wick is drenched.

8.

Kówó kówó	Be felled, be felled[4]
Àràbà kòwó mọ́	The *àràbà* (silk cotton tree) still stands
Ojútì (ì)rókò	The *ìrókò* (African teak tree) is disgraced and confounded
Kówó kówó.	Be felled, be felled.

9.

Ó lé mi ò kàwé o (x2)	He despises me for my illiteracy (x2)
Aláků̀wé ń ṣe lébìrà ní (Ì)kẹjà	Meanwhile many educated people are engaged in labouring jobs[5] in Ìkẹjà[6]
Ó lé mi ò kàwé o	Yet he despises me for my illiteracy
Iṣẹ́ ọwọ́ọ̀ mi mò ń ṣe	I profit from the work of my hand
Ọ̀rọ̀ ìwé kọ́ la wí.	Literacy is not the issue here.

10.

A dá lápá (x2)	It will end up with fractured limbs (x2)
Kọ̀nkọ̀ tó bákèré fò	The bullfrog[7] that tries to out-jump the striped frog
A dá lápá.	Will end up with fractured limbs.

11.

Àwa làgbà (x2)	We are in charge here (x2)
Adìrẹ funfun làgbà adìrẹ	(Just like) the white chicken is in charge of the poultry
Àwa làgbà.	We are in charge.

12.

Àwa yín la nìlú	We are joint heirs to this land (this is my land too)
Ẹ má pè wá lálejò mọ́	Do not call us guests anymore
Àwa yín la nìlú.	We are joint heirs to this land.

13.

Bóbá ti rí ni ẹ wí (x2)	Say it as it is (x2)
Àlá kìí ba ni lérù	A dream can not be so terrifying
Ká má leèrọ	As to prevent the dreamer from relating it
Bóbá ti rí ni ẹ wí.	Say it as it is.

14.

Ọ̀tá mi kò ní gbérí mọ́	My enemies are defeated forever
Pirigidi ma fì (ì)kòkò dé wọn mọ́lẹ̀	Totally, I will cover them with an earthenware pot
Pirigidi, pirigidi, pirigidi	Completely, entirely, from top to bottom,

---

⁴   Translator's note: *Kówó kówó* is a verbal expression of wishes that something should fall. Alternatively it could be translated as 'fall, fall' instead of 'be felled, be felled'.

⁵   Translator's note: The use of the word *lébìrà* (an English loan word from labourer) implies that this *òwe* was developed in colonial or post-colonial times.

⁶   Translator's note: Ìkẹjà was an early industrial town in Nigeria and is now a northern region of Lagos. Mention of Ìkẹjà dates this *òwe* to post-1950s as the Ìkẹjà Industrial Estate was established around that time and it became common for the unemployed to travel there for menial jobs.

⁷   *Kọ̀nkọ̀* and *àkèré* are varieties of frogs. *Àkèré* is a lot more agile and usually jumps much further than *kọ̀nkọ̀*.

Ma fì (ì)kòkò dé wọn mọ́lẹ̀	I will cover them
Pirigidi.	Thoroughly!

15.
Labalábá tó dìgbò lègún	The butterfly that falls upon thorns
Aṣọ rẹ̀ á ya.	Will end up with shredded clothes (wings).

16.
Ẹ fàbùkù kán (x2)	Let them be disgraced (x2)
Ẹni tó bá tọrọ àbùkù	Those who behave disgracefully
Ẹ fàbùkù kán	They deserve to be disgraced
Bẹ́ẹ̀ ni, bẹ́ẹ̀ ni, bẹ́ẹ̀ ni	Yes, yes, yes (It is appropriate and pertinent)
Ẹ fà bùkù kán.	Let them be disgraced.

17.
Kí ní ó fì (ì)bejì ṣẹ (x2)	To what extent can they succeed with Ìbejì[8] (x2)
(Ọmọ Ọdẹ́kúnlé)	(Descendant of Ọdẹ́kúnlé)[9]
Ẹni tí ń kan orí (ì)bejì sínú	Those who attempt to divert the destiny of Ìbejì
Kí ní ó fì (ì)bejì ṣe.	They cannot succeed in the case of Ìbejì.

18.
Ó lè ṣọni nù	They can always turn out to be oppressors
Ẹni tó bá juni lọ	Those who happen to be mightier
Ó lè ṣọni nù.	Can always turn out to be oppressors.

19.
Gbangba làṣá ta (x2)	The hawk soars in the open (x2)
Àṣá kìí ta	The hawk does not soar
Àṣá kìí ta ní kọ̀rọ̀	It does not soar in hiding
Gbangba làṣá ta.	The hawk soars in the open.

20.
Ẹ ṣẹnu bó ṣe wà (x2)	Watch your mouth (x2)
Ẹ má ṣẹnu jáku jàku mọ́	Do not open your mouth unscrupulously
Ẹ ṣẹnu bó ṣe wà.	Watch your mouth.

21.
Babaà mi ló bí mi (x2)	I am a true child of my father (x2)
Èmi kìí ṣọmọkọ́mọ tí baléjẹ́	I am not a deviant that disrupts the family integrity
Babaà mi ló bí mi.	I am a true child of my father.

22.
Àwọn dà?	Where are they?
Àwọn tí ń pe rawọn	Those who falsely ascribe
Ní ǹkan pàtàkì	Importance to themselves
Àwọn dà?	Where are they?
A à rí wọn.	They are nowhere to be found.

---

[8]   The *òrìṣà* of twins.

[9]   Àyándòkun played the text 'Ọmọ Ọdẹ́kúnlé' in the *omele mẹ́ta* performance but not in the *ìyáàlù/omele abo* performance. Ọdẹ́kúnlé is his father's name and can be interpolated virtually anywhere in drummed *òwe* performances.

23.

Èmi ò gbọdọ̀ gbọ mọ́ ọ̀rọ̀ játi jàti	Let no one utter nonsense around me
Mi ò gbọdọ̀ gbọ mọ́	Let no one drag me into useless talk
Ọ̀rọ̀ játi jàti	Nonsense words
Mi ò gbọdọ̀ gbọ mọ́.	Spare your nonsense from now on.

Oríkì
(Examples AII.2–11)

Example AII.2. *Oríkì* Àyàn (⊙ 2 & 12)

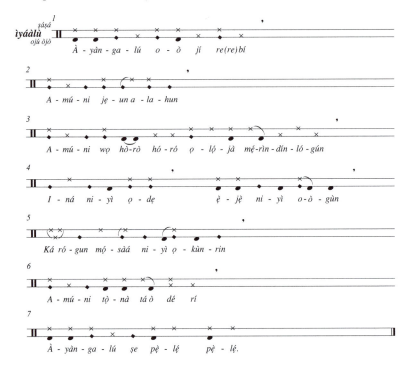

Àyàngalú o ò jí rere bí   I greet you this morning
Amúni jẹun alahun   The one who gives us what it takes to
                                        extract patronage, even from the miserly
Amúni wọ hòrò hóró ọlọ́jà mẹ́rìndínlógún   Leading us into the sixteen innermost secret
                                        places of the market
Iná niyì ọdẹ   The headlamp[10] is the glory of the hunter
Ẹ̀jẹ̀ niyì oògùn   Blood is the glory of medicine
Kárógun mọ́sàá niyì ọkùnrin   Not to be afraid of war is the glory of man
Amúni tọ̀nà tá ò dé rí   He makes one to travel an unknown road
Àyàngalú ṣe pẹ̀lẹ́ pẹ̀lẹ́.   Àyàn Àgalú keep cool.[11]

---

[10]   Translator's note: *Iná* usually means fire or light, but in this context, *iná* refers to a headlamp lit with carbide, which Yorùbá hunters strap to their head. Animals are stupefied when they see the light and the hunters are proud of this efficacious hunting technique.

[11]   *Ṣe pẹ̀lẹ́* is difficult to translate directly and can also be translated as 'stay calm', 'keep a cool head', 'peace' or 'be careful' in the context of the *oríkì* presented in this section.

Example AII.3.   *Oríkì* Ògún (☉ 3)

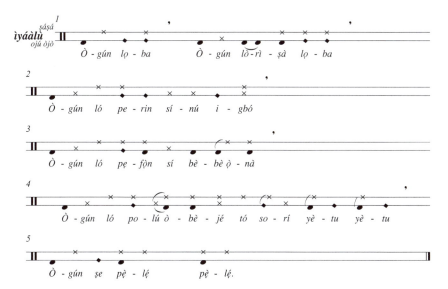

Ògún lọba	Ògún the king
Ògún lòrìṣà lọba	Ògún, both *òrìṣà* and king
Ògún ló perin nínú igbó	It was Ògún who killed an elephant in the forest
Ògún ló pẹfọ̀n si bèbè ọ̀nà	It was Ògún who killed a buffalo/bush cow on the roadside
Ògún ló polú òbèjé tó sorí yètu yètu	It was Ògún who killed the duiker with fluffy hair on its head
Ògún ṣe pẹ̀lẹ́ pẹ̀lẹ́.	Ògún keep cool.

Example AII.4.   *Oríkì* Ọ̀ṣun (⊙ 4)

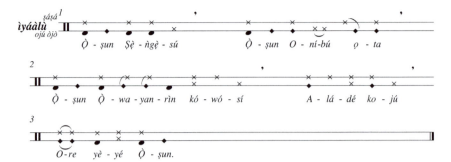

Ọ̀ṣun Ṣẹ̀ngẹ̀sú   Ọ̀ṣun Ṣẹ̀ngẹ̀sú (praise name)
Ọ̀ṣun oníbú ọta   Ọ̀ṣun, guardian of the storehouse of stones
Ọ̀ṣun Ọ̀wayanrìn kówósí   Ọ̀ṣun hides money in the sand
Aládé kojú   (meaning unclear)
Ore yèyé Ọ̀ṣun.   I greet you, great mother.

Example AII.5.   *Oríkì* Ṣàngó (☉ 5)

Àjàlá ìjí ṣe pèlé pèlé
Afójú Àjànàkú kò mọ (i)gi kò mọnìyàn

Àjàlá ìjí mọ́ọ̀ bá mi jà
Mi ò lówó ẹbọ nilé
Àjàlá ìjí wọ ṣòkòtò (ì)jà
Ṣe pèlé.

Àjàlá ìjí (praise name) keep cool
The blind elephant that recognises neither tree nor man
Àjàlá ìjí, do not afflict me
I have no money for sacrifice
Àjàlá ìjí, dressed in war trousers
Keep cool.

Example AII.6.   *Oríkì* Èṣù (☉ 6)

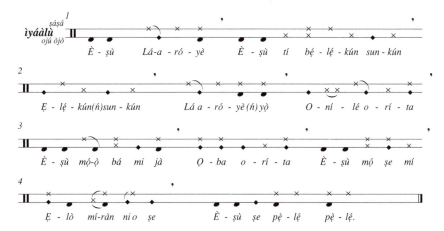

Èṣù Láaróyè
Èṣù tí bẹ́lẹ́kún sunkún
Ẹlẹ́kún ń sunkún
Láaróyè ń yọ̀
Onílé oríta
Èṣù mọ́ọ̀ bá mi jà
Ọba oríta
Èṣù mọ́ ṣe mí
Ẹlò míràn ni o ṣe
Èṣù ṣe pẹ̀lẹ́ pẹ̀lẹ́.

Èṣù Láaróyè (praise name)
Èṣù who weeps with the bereaved
While the bereaved is weeping
Láaróyè is rejoicing
He who inhabits crossroads
Èṣù do not harm me
King of the crossroads
Èṣù, do not harm me
Please, pick on someone else
Èṣù keep cool.

Example AII.7.   *Oríkì* Ọbàtálá (☉ 7)

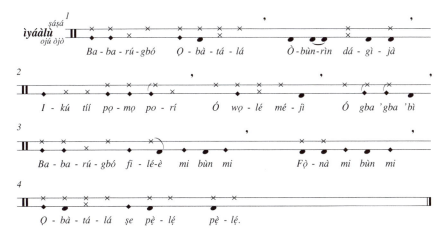

Babarúgbó Ọbàtálá   Ancient father Ọbàtálá
Òbùnrìn dágìjà   Whose gait is characterised by wide strides
Ikú tíí pọmọ porí   Death that kills totally
Ó wọlé méjì   He enters two houses
Ó gba (i)gba (o)bì   He receives two hundred kola nuts
Babarúgbó filéè mi bùn mi   Ancient father, please concede my home to me
Fọ̀nà mi bùn mi   Concede my journeys to me
Ọbàtálá ṣe pẹ̀lẹ́ pẹ̀lẹ́.   Ọbàtálá keep cool.

Example AII.8.   *Oríkì* Òrìṣà Oko (☉ 8)

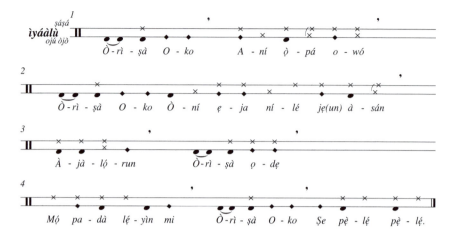

Òrìṣà Oko
Aní ọ̀pá owó

Òrìṣà Oko Òní ẹja nílé jẹun àsán

Àjàlọ́run
Òrìṣà ọdẹ
Mọ́ padà lẹ́yìn mi
Òrìṣà Oko ṣe pẹ̀lẹ́ pẹ̀lẹ́.

Òrìṣà Oko
He who holds a staff decorated with cowrie shells
Òrìṣà Oko, he who has fish at home but chooses to eat food without meat
One whose effect is felt in heaven
Òrìṣà of hunters
Do not withdraw your support from me
Òrìṣà Oko keep cool.

Example AII.9.   *Oríkì* Ṣọ̀pọ̀nnọ́ (☉ 9)

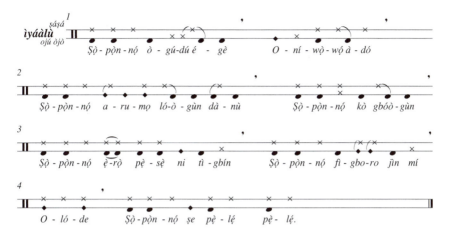

Ṣọ̀pọ̀nnọ́ ògúdú ègè	Ṣọ̀pọ̀nnọ́, full of *ègè*[12]
Oníwọ̀wọ́ àdó	Custodian of several medicine gourds
Ṣọ̀pọ̀nnọ́ arumọ lóògùn dànù	Ṣọ̀pọ̀nnọ́, the one who spoils people's medicines
Ṣọ̀pọ̀nnọ́ kò gbóògùn	Ṣọ̀pọ̀nnọ́ answers to no antidote
Ṣọ̀pọ̀nnọ́ ẹ̀rọ̀ pẹ̀sẹ̀ pẹ̀sẹ̀ ni tìgbín	Ṣọ̀pọ̀nnọ́, the snail epitomises peace and tranquillity
Ṣọ̀pọ̀nnọ́ fìgboro jìn mí	Ṣọ̀pọ̀nnọ́, concede the streets to me
Olóde, Ṣọ̀pọ̀nnọ́ ṣe pẹ̀lẹ́ pẹ̀lẹ́.	Controller of the streets, Ṣọ̀pọ̀nnọ́, stay cool.

---

[12]   Translator's note: *Ègè* is a musical genre common among the Ẹ̀gbá.

Example AII.10.   *Oríkì* Iyemǫja (☉ 10)

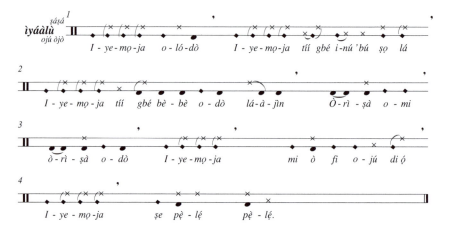

Iyemǫja olódò	Iyemǫja, custodian of the rivers
Iyemǫja tíí gbé inú (i)bú ṣọlá	Iyemǫja, who lives in celebration in the *ibú*[13]
Iyemǫja tíí gbé bèbè odò láàjìn	Iyemǫja, who dwells on the river bank in the dead of night
Òrìṣà omi, òrìṣà odò	The òrìṣà of the waters, the òrìṣà of rivers
Iyemǫja, mi ò fi ojú di ǫ	Iyemǫja, I dare not disrespect you
Iyemǫja ṣe pèlé pèlé.	Iyemǫja, keep cool.

---

13   *Ibú* can be literally translated as 'whirlpool' but has a deeper religious meaning in reference to water *òrìṣà*. The place in the river where the water swirls is considered to be an energy point, and devotees build their shrines at such points. *Ibú* are also dimensions of the water *òrìṣà* (see Barber 1990).

Example AII.11.   *Oríkì* Oya (☉ 11)

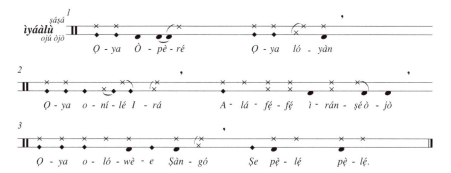

Oya Òpèré	Oya Òpèré (praise name)
Oya lóyàn	It is Oya who succeeds
Oya onílé Irá	Oya, who makes her home in Irá
Aláféfé ìránsé òjò	Oya, controller of the wind, messenger of rain
Oya olówèe Sàngó	Oya, Sàngó's favourite (wife)
Se pèlé pèlé.	Keep cool.

Ìlù Òrìṣà Texts and Translations

Examples A.II.12 through to A.II.20 are audio examples that can be heard on the CD that accompanies this book. The symbol ☉ followed by a number indicates the track number on the CD. For full track listings, please refer to the List of CD Examples.

Example AII.12.   *Ìlù* Ògún (☉ 22)

First text (basic rhythm)
Ṣá di di ṣà di di

"Ògún walks with character"[14]
(*ẹnà* vocables)

Second text (*oríkì*) x2
Ògún fẹrẹ bí onílé

Ògún moves around quickly, like the home owner

Ògún fẹrẹ bí ọlọ́nà

Ògún moves around quickly, as one who owns the road

Ògún dé kùrù kẹrẹ kùrù kẹrẹ kùrù kẹrẹ.

Ògún arrives in a train of activity.

Third text (*oríkì*)
Inú ọjà la ńlọ
Èrò ọjá para mọ́
Inú ọjà la ńlọ.

We head for the market
Those in the market should take heed
We head for the market.

Fourth text (*oríkì*)
Wòrú o Wòrú oko
Wòrú o Wòrú odò
Wòrú pakà féyẹ jẹ
Mo délé morò fún baba
Babá na Wòrú jọjọ
Lábẹ́ ọgẹ̀dẹ̀
Lábẹ́ òrònbó
O ti ṣe dábẹ́ ata?
Idẹ wẹ́rẹ́ ni tỌ̀ṣun
Òjé gùdùgbà ni tÒrìṣà
Ṣẹ́kẹ́ṣẹkẹ̀ ni tÒgún

Wòrú[15] in the farm
Wòrú at the river
Wòrú shelled corn for birds to eat
I returned home to tell father
Father gaveWòrú a serious beating
Under the banana tree
Under the orange tree
How did you end up under the chilli tree?
Brass bits are the symbol of Òṣun
The lead bracelet is that of Òrìṣà (Ọbàtálá)
As for Ògún, it is handcuffs of iron

---

[14]   This is Àyándòkun's translation in inverted commas, although Adégbọlá could not identify any semantic meaning from *Ṣá di di ṣà di di* and concluded that they are drum vocables. In his *dùndún* transcription of the same rhythm, Oyèlámì (1989) wrote, '*sá sá gidi sà sà gidi*'. That different consonants are used by Àyándòkun and Oyèlámì probably confirms Adégbọlá's suggestion that these are non-semantic vocables. The disparity in Àyándòkun's and Oyèlámì's versions also constitutes an example of a difference between *bàtá* and *dùndún* vocables as [g] is not used in *ẹnà bàtá*. It may be that the drum rhythm rendered by the vocables is played for a particular style of Ògún dance, which elicits an association and 'translation' from Àyándòkun.
[15]   Àyándòkun said that Wòrú is 'the singer'.

Ẹ bá mi kìlọ̀ fún baálẹ̀
Kó bá mi módòdó pakájà
Gbogbo wa lÒgún jọbí.

Please enjoin the *baálẹ̀*[16]
To let me have floral material for cothes
After all, we are all offspring of Ògún.

(Return to *Ṣá di di ṣà di di* x 2)

Fifth text (*oríkì*)
Baba gbé ṣàdidi wá
Mi ò rà ni mo wí
Baba gbé ṣàdidi wá
Mi ò rà ni mo wí
Baba gbé ṣàdidi wá.

Baba offers *ṣàdidi*[17] for sale
I declined
Baba offers *ṣàdidi* for sale
I declined
Baba offers *ṣàdidi* for sale.

(Return to *Ṣá di di ṣà di di* x 9)

(Change of rhythm to *àgẹ̀rẹ̀*)

Sixth text (*òwe*)
Ibi ọká bá ba sí, ìrẹ̀ ò gbọdọ̀ han.

The cricket dares not make a sound in the
vicinity of the Gaboon viper.
(The implied meaning is that insignificant
people should not dare the powerful.)

---

[16] *Baálẹ̀* is a chieftancy title in certain towns such as Ògbómọ̀ṣọ́ and Ìbàdàn.
[17] The meaning of *ṣàdidi* in this context is obscure.

Example AII.13. *Ìlù* Ọ̀sun (☉ 23)

Ṣẹṣẹ kúṅdú, ṣẹṣẹ kúṅdú	(Meaning obscure)
Ta ní ń jo?	Who is dancing?
Ọ̀sun ní ń jo	It is Ọ̀sun
Pàra ń ga j̀ga	(Meaning unclear)[18]
Ọ̀sun yèyé.	Ọ̀sun, great mother.

Ṣẹ̀ṣẹ̀ kú ń dú, ṣẹ̀ṣẹ̀ kú ń dú

Wòrú o Wòrú oko	Wòrú in the farm
Wòrú o Wòrú odò	Wòrú at the river
Wòrú pakà fẹ́yẹ jẹ	Wòrú shelled corn for birds to eat
Mo délé morò fún baba	I returned home to tell father
Babá na Wòrú jọjọ	Father gaveWòrú a serious beating
Lábẹ́ ọ̀gẹ̀dẹ̀	Under the banana tree
Lábẹ́ òròńbò	Under the orange tree
O ti ṣe dábẹ́ ata	How did you end up under the chilli tree?
Idẹ wẹ́rẹ́ ni tỌ̀sun	Brass bits are the symbol of Ọ̀sun,
Òjé gùdùgbà ni tỌ̀rìṣà	The lead bracelet is that of *Òrìṣà* (Ọbàtálá)
Ṣẹ́kẹ́ṣẹkẹ̀ ni tÒgún	As for Ògún, it is chains (handcuffs) of iron
Ẹ bá mi kìlọ̀ fún baálẹ̀	Please enjoin the *baálẹ̀*
Kó bá mi módòdó pakájà	To let me have floral material for cothes
Gbogbo wa lÒgún jọbí.	After all, we are all offspring of Ògún.

Ṣẹ̀ṣẹ̀ kú ń dú, ṣẹ̀ṣẹ̀ kú ń dú

Pàra ń ga j̀ga	(Meaning unclear)
Ọ̀sun yèyé.	Ọ̀sun, great mother.

Example AII.14. *Ìlù* Ọya (☉ 24)

Ọya, ògbodò gboko.	Ọya, you who takes over the river and the farm.

Example AII.15. *Ìlù* Ṣàngó (☉ 25)

Àlùsì, Ẹ bá mi tàlùsì jáde	Àlùsì, let us drive out the worthless person
Àfẹni tí kọgílá kọlù	Only a disorientated person
Àfẹni tí Èṣù ńṣe	A person under the spell of Èṣù
Ló lè kọ lÈṣù	Dares confront Èṣù
Ló lè kọ lu Ṣàngó	Dares confront Ṣàngó
Ẹfẹnu mọ́nu	Keep your mouth shut
Ṣàngó dé	Ṣàngó has arrived
Ṣàngó dé.	Ṣàngó has come.

---

[18] Adégbọlá could not extract semantic meaning from *pàra ń ga j̀ga*. Àyándòkun said that *pàra ń ga j̀ga* is 'a kind of Ọ̀sun movement'. Like *ṣá di di ṣà di di* in *Ìlù* Ògún, *pàra ń ga j̀ga* may be non-semantic syllables that are associated with a movement in the ritual dance.

Example AII.16. *Ìlù* Ìbejì (☉ 26)

Mo mú (ì)bejì	I will take twins
Mo mú (ì)bejì relé	I will take twins home
Tere tere yàn lóònìí	They are favoured with goodness today[19]
Ké̩hìndé yàn	Ké̩hìndé is favoured[20]
Táyè lo lú yàn	Táyè survives[21]
È̩jìré̩ yàn lóònìí	The two of them survive today
Ìdòwú yàn lóònìí	Ìdòwú (the child born after the twins) is favoured today
Àlàbá yàn lóònìí.	Àlàbá (the female child born after Ìdòwú) is favoured today).

Example AII.17. *Ìlù* Iyemo̩ja (☉ 27)

Iyemo̩ja, Iyemo̩ja	Iyemo̩ja, Iyemo̩ja
Olódò.	Custodian of the river.

Example AII.18. *Ìlù* O̩bè̩dú (☉ 28)

No known text

Example AII.19. *Ìlù* O̩bàlùfò̩n (☉ 29)

O̩bàlùfò̩n	O̩bàlùfò̩n

Example AII.20. *Ìlù* O̩bàtálá (☉30)

Òrìsà gba (i)gba obì	Òrìsà (O̩bàtálá) took two hundred kola nuts
O̩mo̩ mo wá gbà, O̩bàtálá	O̩bàtálá, I have come to make a request for children
O̩mo̩ mo wá gbà, Bàbárúgbó	It is children I have come to request, ancient father
Ko̩ko̩ ko̩ko̩ bù	(meaning unclear)
Ó wo̩lé méjì	He visits two houses
Ó gbagba (o)bì	He accepts two hundred kola nuts
Gbagba bùrìn bùrìn.	He accepts two hundred and sets out, taking a short cut.

---

[19] Translator's note: *Tere tere* may be non-semantic vocables.

[20] Translator's note: The last word *yàn* implies survival in the sense of meaningful existence. This text as a whole could be viewed as a prayer, drumming, singing and dancing the twins into survival and meaningful existence, given the high mortality rate.

[21] Yorùbá twins are always named Táíwò (nicknamed Táyè - the one that comes first to taste the world) and Ké̩hìndé (the one that comes after). Táyélolú is the full rendition of Táyé, while Ké̩hìndé is a redaction of O̩mo̩ké̩hìndé.

Example AII.21.   *Ìlù* Èṣù (☉ 31)

Èṣù Látọpa	Èṣù, prestigious-person-who-wields-a-club
	(Euba 1990:488)
Èṣù gọngọ.	(Meaning obscure)

Bibliography

Abímbọlá, 'Wándé, *Ifá Will Mend Our Broken World: Thoughts on Yoruba Religion and Culture in Africa and the Diaspora* (Massachusetts: Aim Books, 1997).

——, 'Continuity and Change in the Verbal, Artistic, Ritualistic, and Performance Traditions of Ifa Divination' in John Pemberton III (ed.), *Insight and Artistry in African Divination* (Washington and London: Smithsonian Institution Press, 2000: 175–81).

Abraham, R.C., *Dictionary of Modern Yorùbá* (London: University of London Press, 1958).

Agawu, Kofi, *African Rhythm: A Northern Ewe Perspective* (Cambridge: Cambridge University Press, 1995).

Àjàyí, 'Bade, 'Yoruba Drum Language: A Problem of Interpretation' *Nigeria Magazine* 58.1 (1990): 2.

Amira, John and Steven Cornelius, *The Music of Santería: Traditional Rhythms of the Batá Drums* (Tempe, Arizona: White Cliffs Media Inc., 1991).

Awolalu, J. Omosade, *Yoruba Beliefs and Sacrificial Rites* (Essex, UK: Longman, 1979).

Bankole, Ayo, Judith Bush and Sadek H. Samaan, 'The Yoruba Master Drummer', *African Arts*, 8.2 (1975): 48–56, 77–8.

Barber, Karin, 'How Man Makes God in West Africa: Yoruba Attitudes toward the Orisha' *Africa*, 513 (1981): 724–45.

——, 'Oriki, Women and the Proliferation and Merging of Orisa', *Africa*, 60.3 (1990): 313–337.

——, *I Could Speak until Tomorrow: Oríkì, Women and the Past in a Yorùbá Town* (Edinburgh: Edinburgh University Press, 1991).

Bascom, William, 'Drums of the Yoruba of Nigeria' (sleeve notes) (New York: Folkways Records [LP] #FE4441, 1953)

——, *Ifa Divination: Communication between Gods and Men in West Africa* (Bloomington and Indianapolis: Indiana University Press, 1991 [1969]).

——, *Sixteen Cowries: Yoruba Divination from Africa to the New World* (Bloomington and Indianapolis: Indiana University Press, 1993 [1980]).

Beier, Ulli, 'The Talking Drums of the Yoruba', *African Music Society Journal*, 1 (1954): 29–31.

——, 'Before Odùduwà', *Odu* 3 (1956): 25–32.

Branda-Lacerda, Marcos, *Kultische Trommelmusik der Yoruba in der Volksrepublik Benin - Bata-Sango und Bata-Egungun in der Städten Pobe und Sakété* (Hamburg: Verlag der Musikalienhandlung, Karl Dieter Wagner, 1988).

Cage, John, *M: Writing '67–72* (London: Calder and Boyars, 1973).

Carrington, J.F., 'The Talking Drums of Africa' in Thomas A. Sebeok and Donna Jean Umiker-Sebeok (eds), *Speech Surrogates: Drum and Whistle Systems* (The Hague, Paris: Monton (1976 [1949]).

Clapperton, Hugh, with Richard Lander, *Journal of a Second Expedition into the Interior of Africa from the Bight of Benin to Soccatoo to which is added the Journal of Richard Lander from Kano to the Sea-Coast Partly by a More Easterly Route* (London: Frank Cass & Company Limited, 1966 [1829]).

Cooke, Peter, 'Ganda Xylophone Music: Another Approach', *African Music* 4.4 (1970): 62–80.

Drewal, Henry John, and John Mason, *Beads, Body, and Soul: Art and Light in the Yorùbá Universe* (Los Angeles: UCLA Fowler Museum of Cultural History, 1998).

Drewal, Henry John and John Pemberton III, *Yoruba: Nine Centuries of African Art and Thought* (New York: The Center for African Art in Association with Harry N. Abrams Inc., Publishers, 1989).

Euba, Akin, 'The Interrelationship of Music and Poetry' in 'Wándé Abímbọlá (ed.), *Yorùbá Oral Tradition* (Department of African Languages and Literatures, University of Ilé-Ifẹ̀ African Languages and Literatures Series No. 1 1975).

——, *Yorùbá Drumming: The Dùndún Tradition* (Bayreuth: Bayreuth African Studies, 1990).

Hause, Helen, 'Terms for Musical Instruments in The Sudanic Languages; A Lexicographical Enquiry', *Journal of the American Oriental Society*, Supplement 7, Jan–Mar (1948): 1xviii.

Hughes, David, 'The Historical Uses of Nonsense: Vowel-Pitch Solfege from Scotland to Japan' in Margot Lieth Philipp (ed.), *Ethnomusicology and the Historical Dimension* (Ludwigsburg, Frg: Philipp Verlag, 1989).

——, 'No Nonsense: The Logic and Power of Acoustic-Iconic Mnemonic Systems', *British Journal of Ethnomusicology*, 9.2, (2000): 93–120.

Ìdòwú, E. Bolaji, *Olodumare: God in Yoruba Belief* (Brooklyn, New York: A & B Books Publishers, 1994 [1962]).

Ìṣọlá, Akínwùnmí, 'Ẹna: Code-Talking in Yoruba', *Journal of West African Languages*, 12.1 (1982): 43–51.

——, 'Religious Politics and The Myth of Ṣango' in Jacob Olupona (ed.), *African Traditional Religions in Contemporary Society* (New York: Paragon House, 1991).

Johnson, Rev. Samuel, *The History of the Yorubas* (Lagos: C.S. Bookshops, 1976 [1921]).

King, Anthony V., 'Employments of the "Standard Pattern" in Yoruba Music', *African Music*, 2.3 (1960): 51–4.

——, *Yoruba Sacred Music from Ekiti* (Ibadan: University Press, 1961).

Klein, Debra L., *Yoruba Bàtá: Politics of Pop Tradition in Ẹ̀rìn-Ọ̀ṣun and Overseas* (PhD Dissertation, University of California, Santa Cruz, 2000).

——, *Yorùbá Bàtá Goes Global* (Chicago and London: The University of Chicago Press, 2007).

Koetting, James, 'Analysis and Notation of West African Drum Ensemble Music', *Selected Reports in Ethnomusicology* 1 (1970): 115–46.

Kubik, Gerhard, *Africa and the Blues* (Jackson, MS: University of Mississippi Press, 1999).

Lander, John and Richard, *The Niger Journal of Richard and John Lander* (New York: Frederick A. Praeger, 1965 [1832]).

Láoyè I, Tìmì Of Ẹdẹ, 'Yoruba Drums', *Odu*, 7 (1959): 5–14.

——, 'Music of Western Nigeria: Origin and Use', *Composer*, 19 (1966): 34–41.

Law, Robin C.C., 'Ethnicity and the Slave Trade: "Lucumi" and "Nago" as Ethnonyms in West Africa', *History in Africa*, 24 (1997): 205–19.

Locke, David and Godwin Kwasi Agbeli, 'A Study of the Drum Language in Adzogbo', *African Music*, 6.1 (1980): 32–52.

Lucas, J., *The Religion of the Yorùbás: Being an Account of the Religious Beliefs and Practices of the Yorùbá Peoples of Southern Nigeria, Especially in Relation to the Religion of Ancient Egypt* (Brooklyn: Athenia Henrietta Press, Inc., 1996 [1948]).

Marcuzzi, Michael D., 'Mimesis and Coding in Yorùbá Bàtá Drumming' conference paper, *Annual Meeting for the Society for Ethnomusicology*, Tucson, AZ, November 5 (2004).

——, *A Historical Study of the Ascendant Role of Bàtá Drumming in Cuban Òrìṣà Worship* (PhD Dissertation, York University, Toronto, 2005).

Nketia, J.H. Kwabena, 'Drumming in Akan Communities' in Thomas A. Sebeok and Donna Jean Umiker-Sebeok (eds), *Speech Surrogates: Drum and Whistle Systems* (The Hague, Paris: Monton, 1976).

——, 'Musicology and Linguistics: Integrating the Phraseology of Text and Tune in the Creative Process', *Black Music Research Journal* 22:2 (2002): 143–64.

Ọládàpọ̀, Ọlátúbọ̀sún, *Àyàn-Akéwì Afìlùsọ̀rọ̀* (Ìbàdàn: Ọlátúbọ̀sún Ọládàpọ̀, 1995).

Omíbíyìí, Mosunmọla, 'The Training of Yoruba Traditional Musicians' in 'Wándé Abímbọ́lá (ed.), *Yoruba Oral Tradition: Poetry in Music, Dance and Drama* (Department of African Languages and Literatures, University of Ilé-Ifẹ̀ African Languages and Literatures Series no. 1, 1978).

Ortiz, Fernando, *Los Instrumentos de la Música Afrocubana, Vol. 4.* (Havana Publicaciones de la Dirección de Cultura del Ministerio de Educación, 1955).

Oyèlámì, Múráínà, *Yorùbá Dùndún Music: A New Notation with Basic Exercise & Five Yorùbá Drum Repertoires* (Bayreuth, Germany: Iwalewa House, 1989).

——, *Yorùbá Bàtá Music: A New Notation with Basic Exercises and Ensemble Pieces* (Bayreuth, Germany: Iwalewa House, 1991).

Palmié, Stephan, 'Introduction: Out of Africa?', *Journal of Religion in Africa*, 37.2 (2007): 159–73.

Peel, John, 'The Pastor and The Babalawo: The Interaction of Religions in Nineteenth-Century Yorubaland', *Africa*, 60.3 (1990): 338–69.

——, *Religious Encounter and The Making of the Yoruba* (Bloomington and Indianapolis: Indiana University Press, 2000).

——, 'Gender in Yoruba Religious Change', *Journal of Religion in Africa*, 322 (2002): 135–66.

Rattray, R.S., 'The Drum Languages of West Africa', *Journal of The African Society*, 22 (1923): 302.

Roberts, John Storm, *Black Music of Two Worlds* (New York: Original Music, 1972).

Rouget, Gilbert, 'Notes et Documents pour Servir À L'étude de la Musique Yoruba', *Journal de la Société des Africansistes*, 35.1 (1965): 67–107.

Sebeok, Thomas A. and Donna Jean Umiker-Sebeok, (eds) *Speech Surrogates: Drum and Whistle Systems* (The Hague, Paris: Monton, 1976).

Smith, Robert S., *The Kingdoms of the Yoruba* (Madison, WI: University of Wisconsin Press, 1988 [1969]).

Stapleton, Chris and Chris May, *African All-Stars: The Pop Music of a Continent* (London and New York: Quartet Books, 1987).

Stern, Theodore, 'Drum and Whistle Languages: An Analysis of Speech Surrogate', *American Anthropologist*, 59.3 (1957): 487–506.

Thieme, Darius L., *A Descriptive Catalogue of Yoruba Musical Instruments* (PhD Dissertation, Catholic University of America, Washington D.C., 1969).

Thompson, Robert Farris, *Flash of the Spirit: African and Afro-American Art and Philosophy* (New York: Vintage Books, 1983).

——, *Face of the Gods: Art and Altars of Africa and the African Americas* (Munich: Prestel, 1993).

Vansina, Jan, *Oral Tradition as History* (Madison: University of Wisconsin Press, 1985).

Vincent [Villepastour], Amanda, *Bata Conversations: Guardianship and Entitlement Narratives about the Bata in Nigeria and Cuba* (PhD Dissertation, School of Oriental and African Studies, University of London, London 2006).

Waterman, Christopher, 'Our Tradition is a Very Modern Tradition: Popular Music and the Construction of Pan-Yoruba Identity', *Ethnomusicology*, 34.3 (1990a): 367–79.

——, *Jùjú: A Social History and Ethnography of an African Popular Music* (Chicago and London: The University of Chicago Press, 1990b).

Wenger, Susan, and Gert Chesi, *A Life with the Gods in their Yorùbá Homeland* (Verlag, Austria: Perlinger, 1983).

Discography

AyanAgalú (2001), Graviton Records.

Drums of the Yoruba of Nigeria (1953), Folkways Records (LP), New York. #FE4441.

Festival of Deities, 'Fátúnmişe, Chief Bólú (n.d.), Ifa Orisa Records.

Okuta Percussion (1992), Haus der Kulturen der Welt. SM1504-2.

Okuta Percussion (featuring Woļé Şoyínká) (1994): *Osika*. Arc Music. YG401.

Oriki de Sango (?) Museo de la Homme, Journal de Africanist 34.

Out of Cuba: Latin American Music Takes Africa by Storm (2005), Topic Records. CDU6862031.

Yoruba Bata Drums – *Elewe Music and Dance* (1980), Folkways Records, Smithsonian Folkways. F-4294.

The Yoruba/Dahomean Collection (1998) – *Orishas Across the Ocean*. The Library of Congress Endangered Music Project. RCD10405.

Yoruba Drums from Benin, West Africa (1996), Smithsonian/Folkways. SF40440.

Index